THE CAMPUS SURVIVAL COOKBOOK #2

+ +

Maybe you never learned to cook because . . .

You haven't got the thyme?
OR
You're convinced hash is only for dopes?
OR
Whipping potatoes seems cruel?
OR
Separating eggs is sad?
OR
Beating the whites is unfair to majorities?
OR
Antipasto sounds bigotted?
OR
Getting into the sauce makes your head ache?
OR
Reducing stock sounds too financial?
OR
Squeezing a lemon sounds like last night's date?

READ ON! . . .

All the mint isn't at Fort Knox!
Keep bread in your pocket!
Use your bean!
Cook with gas!
SURVIVE!

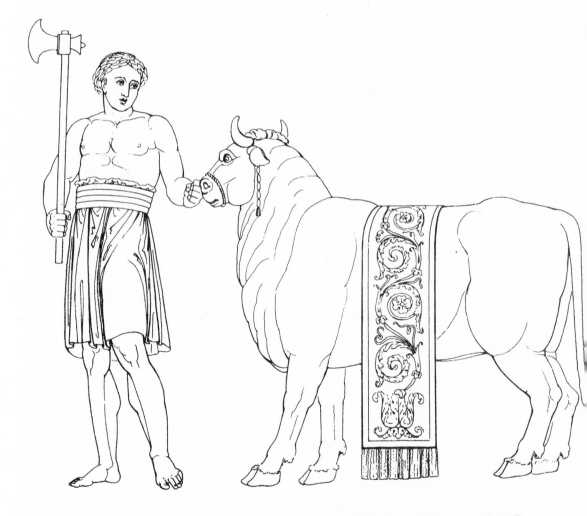

When someone suggests a picnic in the park and asks you to "bring something" . . .

SUMMER SESSION (page 118)

+ + + + + + + + + + + +

THE CAMPUS

SURVIVAL COOKBOOK #2

Got together again by
McCrystle, Sean, and Mike's mother
& Stephanie, Chris, and Jonathan's mother

JACQUELINE WOOD &
JOELYN SCOTT GILCHRIST

Ingeniously illustrated with
leftovers from a course
in art appreciation

QUILL

New York   1981

Library of Congress Cataloging in Publication Data

Wood, Jacqueline.
  The campus survival cookbook #2.

  "Morrow quill paperbacks."

  Includes index.
  1. Cookery. I. Gilchrist, Joelyn Scott.
II. Title.
TX715.W88242   641.5   81-38387
ISBN 0-688-00591-8   AACR2
ISBN 0-688-00568-3 (pbk.)

Printed in the United States of America

3 4 5 6 7 8 9 10

This book is dedicated, with love and admiration,
by each author to the other for having steadfastly
worked so hard, inventing, combining, extemporizing
(and cooking!); traveled thousands of miles to and
fro to get it all together; and gained and lost
117 pounds eating every food herein contained . . .

. . . and by the little fellow, Stone Age Man,
of The Campus Survival Cookbook #1, to the other
little fellow, Technological Genius, SURVIVAL
mascot of Cookbook #2

We will assume you have never seen one before.

YOUR STOVE (page 14)
+ + + + + + + + + + + + +

CONTENTS

+ SURVIVAL—1980s STYLE + 8

+ WHAT SHOULD YOU PUT IN YOUR KITCHEN? + 9
Things to Cook In 9
Things to Eat With 10
Things to Cook With 10
Non-Essential Essentials 14
Should You Get????? 14
Your Stove 14
How to Clean Up 15

+ CUTTING UP + 16

+ ON FREEZING & THAWING + 17

+ HOW TO SELECT MEATS + 19

Dick and Jane 19

+ SHOPPING + 21

+ ANCIENT MAYAN SECRET
  REVEALED + 22

+ FIRST WEEK + Menus 26

Monday 27   Thursday 34
Tuesday 29   Friday 35
Wednesday 32   Saturday 38

+ SECOND WEEK + Menus 40

Monday 41   Thursday 49
Tuesday 43   Friday 50
Wednesday 46   Saturday 52

+ THIRD WEEK + Menus 55

Monday 56   Thursday 60
Tuesday 58   Friday 62
Wednesday 59   Saturday 64

+ FOURTH WEEK + Menus 66

Monday 67   Thursday 72
Tuesday 69   Friday 74
Wednesday 70   Saturday 75

+ JUST DESSERTS + 77

+ ALWAYS ON SUNDAY + 84

+ EL CHEEPO PARTIES + 88

Party Menu #1 88   Party Menu #5   99
Party Menu #2 91   Party Menu #6 100
Party Menu #3 95   Party Menu #7 102
Party Menu #4 97

+ BREADS + 104

+ BIG MEAL SOUPS + 106

+ CRAM-ITS + 113

+ SUMMER SESSION + 118

+ POST GRADUATE + 133

Roasting Everything 133
Sauces! and Gravy! 136
Woking It 138
Blending It 140
International Trio—Classics 143
Three Post Graduate Recipes, SURVIVAL Style 146

+ BY POPULAR DEMAND + 148

+ COOKING TERMS + 155

+ RECIPE INDEX + 156

+ HOW TO FIGURE KITCHEN
  MEASUREMENTS + 160

SURVIVAL—1980s STYLE

WHAT'S GOING ON? Your best friend seems determined to O.D. on yogurt. His girl friend says all dairy products are lethal to anyone over the age of three. The guy next door is fervently stirring mung sprouts in the wok. There's a fiery new spirit of evangelism in three meals a day. Meanwhile there's you, maybe, munching the Fr. Fr. Pots with ketchup.

Who's right?

The truth is that there is no one diet perfect for all. A straight vegetarian diet is weakening for some, especially young people. Yogurt does reproduce helpful B vitamins in the intestinal tract, but it is also a very expensive glass of milk. Certainly take vitamins, learn all you can about them. Clue in to yourself. Unfortunately, since you're unique, you have to learn about yourself, yourself.

You're much more sophisticated about food than students were in 1973, when SURVIVAL #1 was published. Since then, air travel has reduced the world to the size of a grape, and foods which once sounded obscure, even barbaric, are now commonly sold in the local diner: Pita bread, quiches, pilafs, enchiladas are among these. Therefore you'll find them all here too.

But you won't find everything here - not potato-skin chowder, braised sheep testicles, or macrobiotics. One has to draw a line somewhere. Our line is here: There's nothing in this book just because it's good for you. It tastes good too.

This is a book of classy basics for educated people who don't know how to cook but are forced into the kitchen but also lack time and money. The 4 weeks of menus offer well-balanced, delicious meals which you can afford; 4 days of each week are protein-rich but meatless. If you follow it all through, compulsively, day by day, you'll find you actually know how to cook. You've had a crash course in cooking. The POST GRADUATE and EL CHEEPO PARTIES sections will give you credits toward a culinary master's degree.

Never shop when you're hungry or you're liable to buy everything in sight, go over the budget. Try to shop as seldom as possible. Thursday's a good day; meats and vegetables are fresher and the weekend crush hasn't begun.

All daily meals are planned for 2 people. But which 2? Athletes or scholars? Men or women? We thought it best to zero in on 2 normally hungry men. A pair who eat less should cut back on quantities, or learn to use leftovers promptly.

Please read the next pages, which suggest exact utensils for your empty kitchen and also describe a professional technique for slicing and chopping which will slash preparation time to a fraction. Many people who hate to cook simply never learned to speed it up by preparing things quickly - like onions. But your young, clever hands can learn this once and for all time. Try it.

Cooking isn't an inborn talent or genetic characteristic. It's taught. You'll be enchanted with yourself if you do it well, for this skill will prop you up on still another side. You can nonchalantly take over in someone else's kitchen, make gravy, even poach an egg! Cooking is a tremendous social asset.

WHAT SHOULD YOU PUT IN YOUR KITCHEN?

YOU PROBABLY HAVE a "minimum" kitchen. This has been defined as an area in which, if you have to faint, you'd better aim at the doorway. However, these can often be made to work even better than a large space. The pullman kitchens on trains were closets which turned out culinary masterpieces for hundreds of people daily. It depends on what you put in the kitchen, and where.

The handiest item can be a permanent can or pot in which you stuff all the <u>nonsharp</u> tools used daily. You'll never have to search for measuring spoons or ladles if they're right on the counter in front of you. These arrangements also add a definite Gallic panache and will make you look, and feel, as though you know what you're doing.

If you have too few cabinets and drawers, hang pans on hooks on pegboard. If your walls are full, look up. The ceiling has a new world of space possibilities if it's high enough to avoid brain damage. Be ingenious.

Here is a list of minimum utensils for every recipe in this book.

+ <u>THINGS TO COOK IN</u> +

Cheap, thin-bottom pans will drive you crazy. They dent easily, cook unevenly, burn food; next the handles fall off. Get the best <u>aluminum or stainless steel</u> you can afford. Forget the copper-bottom type; these are expensive, cook no better, and they make the whole place look tacky if they're not continuously polished. Get:

A 4-quart aluminum pot for spaghetti and soups and stews. <u>With a lid.</u>

THREE saucepans. Most important, the <u>2-quart size</u>; it will be in <u>constant</u> use. As soon as possible, acquire also the 1½-quart and the <u>3-quart</u> sizes. Get in aluminum or steel, and <u>ALL with lids.</u>

A Pyrex casserole, with lid, 1 ½-quart size. This goes into the oven, <u>cannot</u> be used on stove burner.

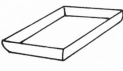

An open roasting pan, about 13" × 9" × 2". You'll use this a lot, so get the heaviest you can afford, and one with a smooth bottom, not grooved. You'll make gravy in this often, plus some cakes.

Get a <u>cheap rack</u> to fit just inside the roasting pan, so meats won't sit in their own grease while cooking. Also use rack on the counter, to set pies and cakes on for proper cooling.

Iron skillets are the patient, stoic heart of the kitchen. They're cheap, homely, reliable. You'll see rows of them hanging in every professional kitchen. (They keep food hot and add a nice rustic touch to a buffet table.) Take care of them and they can be part of your child's dowry. CARE: After each use, add a small amount of water to the pan, boil briefly. Most residue will loosen. When clean and very dry, rub inside with a drop or two of cooking oil to coat. Wipe off excess. This quick procedure ensures a ready, nonstick pan next time. Keep a paper towel between skillets when stacking them. P.S. You get a nutritional bonus when you cook in iron. It adds a considerable percentage of iron to your diet.

A large, 12″ iron skillet. Get a close-fitting lid also.

An 8″ iron skillet for eggs, etc. With a lid.

A square aluminum cake pan, 9″ × 9″.

A 9″ pie pan, aluminum or Pyrex.

A bread loaf pan, about 9″ × 5″. Don't panic. This is for meat loaf and many other things.

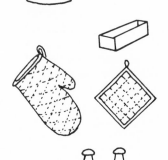

Two potholders are essential. Get the heaviest, padded ones, not the woven type you used to make in kindergarten.

Salt and pepper shakers are in the grocery store.

A toaster. An older, repaired model often has more stamina than a new one.

+ THINGS TO EAT WITH +

A set of dishes. Mix-match castoffs from the Salvation Army or similar junk store can be fun, if judiciously selected.

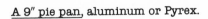

Mugs, glasses. Ditto.

A set of stainless tableware for 8.

+ THINGS TO COOK WITH +

Sharp knives are Numero Uno. Far more gore is caused by trying to hack with a dull knife than clean slicing with a sharp one. Buy only <u>carbon steel</u>, which is soft enough to take a razor edge. Stainless knives get dull and remain so. The carbon knives will darken from acids, etc. That's OK. Just keep them dry.

1. <u>A carbon steel paring knife</u> with 3″ blade. It should feel well balanced in your hand.

2. For larger cutting jobs, look for one with a 6″ blade and a 4 ½″ handle.

<u>A knife sharpener made of ceramic</u>, about 6″ long. These look like little round-ended screwdrivers and are cheap, safe, the best. Holding the angled knife steady in one hand, you lightly stroke the ceramic stick up and down along the blade edge with the other hand. Because you move the sharpener, <u>not</u> the knife, it is safe and quick.

<u>Vegetable peeler</u>, the swivel type. The greatest cheap invention of all time.

<u>Metal measuring spoons</u>. They don't break or melt if left near heat.

<u>Long-handled wooden spoons</u> won't conduct heat, won't burn fingers - or tongues. You can let them stand in the pot.

A cheap <u>cooking utensil set</u>: long-handled fork, spoon, spatula.

<u>A slotted spoon</u> serves vegetables, leaving liquid in the pot.

<u>A slotted spatula</u> flips hamburgers and bacon, dropping grease back into the skillet.

<u>A wire whisk</u> beats eggs and batters and is invaluable for smoothing lumps out of gravies.

<u>A strainer or sieve</u>, plastic or metal, will drain spaghetti, vegetables, and lettuce.

<u>A wooden chopping board</u>, about 10″ × 12″, will protect counter tops, help you get back that security deposit on the apartment. Put it in a handy spot.

<u>Get a bottle/can opener combination</u>. Not electric.

Eventually, POST GRADUATE cooks begin to crave a little extra equipment.

++

A 16-oz. (2-cup) Pyrex measuring cup will accept boiling liquid without breaking. You measure by the see-through method.

A set of mixing bowls, Pyrex here too. You can reheat things in them in the oven.

+ NON-ESSENTIAL ESSENTIALS +

Rubber spatula
Pitcher for frozen juices, with a lid, about 5-cup size
Coffee pot
Cookie sheet
Potato ricer (if you want superior mashed potatoes)
Egg beater, rotary
Vegetable steamer (sits in a pot above the water)
Blender (Many JUST DESSERTS and POST GRADUATE recipes call for this.)
Cheese grater (The 4-sided type doesn't slip on the counter.)
Garlic press (You don't really have to peel the garlic to use this.)
A lettuce drier (Spins water out of greens with centrifugal force, producing paper-dry lettuce in seconds.)
Brush to oil meats, pans. A fancy pastry brush is absurd; get a small, cheap paintbrush at the hardware store.
Spatter shield, a large mesh circle with a handle; screens spatter and keeps stove clean.

+ SHOULD YOU GET????? +

?A crockpot?
We have never tasted a mixture emerging from one of these that didn't remind us of seething primordial ooze. Try it first. Borrow one.

?Teflon-lined pans?
They're making this stuff better and better, but we still wouldn't recommend Teflon-lined pans in daily use. This material scars too easily unless you handle with saintly care and use only plastic utensils.

?An electric skillet?
Weigh these points. GOOD: "Low" heat is well controlled, so there's little chance of burning food. They'll keep food hot, without overcooking, on a buffet. BAD: They take up a lot of space, are very awkward to store. The electric cords always seem too short, so you end up cooking on the floor or radiator. GOOD: They're usually easy to clean. BAD: On "medium" and "high" heat, you have to stand over them, regulating temperature.

+ YOUR STOVE +

We will assume you have just emerged from the trackless wastes of the Gobi and have never seen one before.

<u>On stove top</u>: Boil, simmer, fry, and sauté, in saucepans and skillets.

<u>In oven, if ELECTRIC stove</u>: Bake and roast with <u>bottom</u> heating element, door closed.

<u>Broil</u> with <u>top</u> heating element, oven rack 7″ away from heat, <u>door ajar.</u>

<u>In oven, if GAS stove</u>: Bake or roast, door closed.

<u>Broil</u> in bottom unit ("drawer") with rack or broiling pan 5″ from heat, <u>unit closed</u>.

N.B. <u>Accurate oven temperatures</u> are very important. A difference of twenty-five degrees or so can produce disasters. Generally, your local gas and electric company repairman will check your oven's accuracy for free.

+ <u>HOW TO CLEAN UP</u> +

You have to strike like a cobra. <u>Instantly</u> put used utensils in a pan of sudsy water to soak; they'll clean themselves. If you're having a party and want to do dishes later, rinse plates before stacking - unless you feel up to scrubbing <u>both</u> sides later. Get:

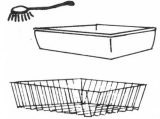

<u>A long-handled sink brush with stiff bristles</u>: (keeps your hands out of water) and a <u>small plastic dishpan</u> to soak things in.

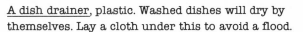

<u>A dish drainer</u>, plastic. Washed dishes will dry by themselves. Lay a cloth under this to avoid a flood.

<u>Six cloth towels, preferably cotton</u>. You can reuse these all year; throw them in with the wash. Economy note: One large roll of paper towels can cost as much as half a chicken; use them sparingly. Ecology note: Save a tree!

A college friend was puzzled by the poisonous-sweet smell haunting his apartment. Trained sleuthwork led to his kitchen trash can with one of those easy-to-push-open tops. NOT practical. <u>Get a tough 6-gallon plastic can with a lid that clamps shut</u>. You should empty the can daily, but you probably won't. <u>Always line the can with plastic bags or a grocery sack</u> folded back at the top - this makes a larger target area; hauling out the bag is easier and cleaner than dumping out the can.

<u>Grease can</u>. MUST have, but it's not something you buy. Use fruit-juice can, coffee can (good - has a lid), any can, and ALWAYS pour excess grease from bacon, sausage (we usually tell you when) into it. Pouring grease into sink makes a terrible mess and does even worse things to the plumbing.

CUTTING UP

THERE IS PRESENTLY a fashionable woman in Connecticut with a happy husband. Each day she runs around doing good deeds and playing tennis and bridge until too late. Speeding home at 5:30, she immediately puts on an apron, chops an onion, and throws it into a frying pan with some butter. In seconds her husband strolls in and exclaims with admiration, "That smells delicious!" He thinks she has been standing over a hot stove all day, thinking only of him.

MORAL: The way to chop an onion is FAST.

Round objects are easy to chop and slice if you first cut them in half. This is the secret of the wizard-speed you wonder at on TV cooking shows.

+ TO SLICE AN ONION +

1. Use your longer <u>sharp</u> knife, a peeled onion, a chopping board.
2. Cut it in half, top to bottom, <u>through the root</u>.
3. Place it flat side down on board.
4. Slice through the <u>width</u>, as thin as you want.

+ TO CHOP AN ONION +

1. Cut peeled onion in half, as above.
2. If right-handed, point root to left, hold down with left hand.
3. With right hand, point knife tip toward root. Make many thin slices lengthwise, but not quite through the root - the root will hold everything together.
4. Make many fine slices <u>across</u> the slices already made. The onion will now fall into small dice.

+ <u>COMMENTS</u> +

1. An onion is easier to <u>peel</u> if you soak it in a bowl of hot tap water for 1-2 minutes.
2. The part of the onion that makes you cry is the <u>root</u>. Keep it intact. Throw it away.

+ TO CHOP GARLIC CLOVE +

You can do this right over the pan if you're careful.

1. Peel it. Make many deep crosshatch slices down the clove, then slice across. Chip the root into tiny pieces.
2. Chefstyle crushed garlic: Don't peel. Put clove on wooden board. Slap it hard with a large knife, blade laid flat. BANG! The skin slips off and the garlic is mashed to a pulp.

+ <u>TO CHOP SCALLIONS</u> +

Trim off root end and about ⅓ of green tops (test to find tender point in the green). Lay scallions on wooden surface. Slit end to end with tip of sharp pointed knife. Align strips of slit scallions. Cut across at ¼" intervals. Scallions are now "chopped."

+ OH, ¶$%S§&*H°¶I§$%T!!! - OR: I FORGOT TO THAW THE MEAT +

FIRST ARE some techniques for cooking frozen meats when time is short. COMMENTS and other items which follow give you a general discussion of the subject.

+ COOKING FROZEN STEAKS, CHOPS +

Tender steaks and chops are excellent broiled while still frozen, and many people prefer this method because juices seem to remain inside.

Coat meat liberally on both sides with cooking oil. It will get a glossy, satin sheen. Broil on one side about 8″ from heat until brown.

Remove from broiler, turn frozen side up, and let sit on counter 10 or 15 minutes. Rising heat will help thaw the top. Return to broiler to brown other side. Remove from oven. Test interior for doneness by making a 1″ slash somewhere in the center. A thick steak may need further broiling at a lower temperature.

When done almost to your liking, remove from broiler, let meat sit on counter for 5 to 10 minutes - it will continue to cook and the cooler air will seal juices.

Remove to hot platter, add butter, salt, and pepper.

+ FROZEN BURGER LOAF IN 45 MINUTES +

Serves 2-3. Thawing is part of the recipe, no time lost.

INGREDIENTS:

1 lb. frozen ground beef	½ cup sour cream
1 cup dry bread crumbs	1 egg, beaten
⅓ package onion-soup mix	¼ teaspoon pepper (no salt)

Put frozen beef in 12″ skillet without any fat. Cover, place over low heat. After 10-15 minutes, you can start to break it up. Stir to separate the cooked part, continue stirring at intervals until it all comes apart. This will take about 30 minutes if meat is frozen in bulk, 15 minutes if frozen in patties. Meat should not brown, just turn grey.

Meanwhile, preheat oven to 500.

Pour off fat in skillet. In bowl, combine meat with other ingredients, breaking up any lumps. Pat into loaf shape, put into loaf pan. Bake at 500 for 15 minutes.

+ COMMENTS ON FREEZING AND THAWING +

Where does the frost in your freezer come from?

Mostly, from what's stored in it. This frost is actually composed of crystals of moisture drawn from the food itself. Dehydration is a principle of freezing.

Because your freezer is probably a small top unit of your refrigerator, holding ice cubes, ice cream, etc., it's opened often, letting in warm air which reduces the efficiency.

For this reason, we don't include an elaborate chapter on freezing foods. You have neither the space nor the separate large unit which would make this practical. Certainly it makes sense to double favorite recipes, freezing half, for future dinners. Throughout the book we have noted which recipes freeze well.

But we suggest all frozen items be eaten within 2 to 4 weeks of storing, especially in summer, or in warm areas. Uncooked meats held too long may even look dry, pale, and stringy; this is freezer burn, which makes meats tough, strange-tasting, even inedible. Poor labeling can cause you to leave foods untouched for too long.

+ TO WRAP AND LABEL FOR FREEZING +

Ladle soups, stews, and casserole mixtures in 2 layers of plastic bags. Between the bags, slide a clearly visible slip of paper noting contents, the date, how many you think it will feed. This information should be written in pencil - ink might frost up and fade. (This labeling is a must, or you'll forget what's in the package and let it sit too long.) Squeeze out all possible air, tie the bag tightly with a plastic strip from the box.

Put the tied bag into the pan or ovenproof dish in which you plan to reheat it. Freeze the food in it. It will take this shape. Tomorrow, remove the pan. Leave bag in freezer. Now, when you want to use the food you have a pan which it fits exactly.

To use food: Remove bags, reheat slowly in original-size pan. For best results, start thawing in 300 oven, then remove to stove top if you like.

+ TO FREEZE COOKED OR RAW MEATS +

Cover air-tight with aluminum foil, pressing out as much air as possible. Put this package into a larger plastic bag with labeling piece of paper inside the plastic, noting contents, date, etc. Place package flat in freezer. It is very hard to cook a piece of frozen, curled up meat.

+ TO KEEP ICE CREAM, SHERBET +

Don't leave them out of the freezer too long when serving. Cover remainder with plastic touching the ice cream, to exclude air. (If frozen to consistency of quarry rock, soften in refrigerator 1-2 hours.)

+ THAWING THINGS, LIKE CHICKEN +

1. Best: In the refrigerator, overnight.
2. Second best: Unwrapped, at room temperature, 3-5 hours.
3. At wit's end: Thaw in waterproof bags in cold water in the sink.
Each of these processes successively draws a little more moisture out of the food.
To thaw fish, see page 36.

+ IF YOU DON'T HAVE A SEPARATE FREEZING SECTION +

If all you have is the small section which holds ice cube trays, frozen food should not be kept for more than a few days. The freezing energy in this small compartment can't do much more than make ice.

HOW TO SELECT MEATS

+ <u>ASK THE BUTCHER</u> +

AH! TO BE A BUTCHER! This dangerous work must be far more tranquilizing - and certainly pays better - than the primal scream, for one seldom meets a depressed or maladjusted meat man.

In the small shops you can observe them, aprons streaked with blood, slicing and grinding, stabbing and pounding, flinging bones into the sawdust! Then they arrange the treasures in the case.

These men are happy! They're ready to communicate. <u>Ask them</u> what cut is best for your recipe, what quantity you need, what temperature to cook it at, how long. Unless the shop is crowded, they'll answer you, joke with you, remember you the next time you come in. If you meet an uncooperative, angry butcher, you are looking at a person with severe problems. Be kind.

+ +
DICK AND JANE - DICK AND JANE - DICK AND JANE - DICK AND JANE - DICK AND -
+ +

+ <u>MEANWHILE, BACK AT THE FARM</u> +

"LOOK! Oh, look!" cried Grandma. "It's Dick and Jane, home from college."

"Hello, Dick, hello, Jane," said Grampa as the big youngsters jumped out of the Porsche.

"Cool!" Jane exclaimed, peering around the large weedy yard. "I want to feed the chickens! Why don't they run around pecking at seeds and things the way they used to?"

Grampa frowned. "Run around! You crazy?" He hauled up his Cardin jeans and spat. "Costs too much. You let 'em run around and they get skinny little drumsticks. <u>Chickens</u> live in the city now. There's a man downtown who raises 'em in a big building with a zillion floors." He shook his head with admiration. "Feet never hit the ground! People pay a lot for the <u>fat</u> on those chickens!"

Dick pulled Jane by the hand, jumping with excitement. "This blows my mind. Let's all go see the animals over in that field!"

"I'll stay here and mind the house." Grandma smiled sweetly. "You never know who'll drop by. People will buy most anything that's old these days."

So Jane and Dick and Grampa climbed the old fence of the pasture. A big steer wandered over.*

"Don't be afraid, Jane," Dick called. Dick showed he wasn't afraid by touching the animal's furry back, right on the center top. Eyes wide, he asked, "What do you call this part, Grampa?"

Jane looked into the steer's soft brown eyes. "What's his name?" she asked.

Grampa shot her a look of disgust and turned to Dick. "Son, college has done you some good, anyway. You got your hand right there on the <u>Tenderloin</u>. <u>Tenderloin</u> is a

---

*In the world of Dick and Jane, the cattle are very docile; they just stand there on the printed page, so to speak.

soft muscle that's as sweet as cake 'cause it runs right along the spine and this critter can't use it much. This is the most expensive part."

Dick shook his head. "Grampa, man, this really blows me away."

Grampa beamed. "And looky here! Right next to the <u>Tenderloin</u> is the <u>Sirloin</u>, which is almost as tender." He stroked the beast's center side and you could tell he was deeply affected.

Just then Grandma came up with an eager young man who began to knock down the old gray fence and haul it away. Grampa didn't seem to notice. He thumped the beast's side and his eyes misted. He spoke softly. "This is where the <u>Standing Rib Roast</u> comes from, these ribs right here." He was visibly moved: "This whole center section is going to cost a fortune all packaged up."

It was an emotional moment, but Jane broke the spell as she danced out of the way of the animal's swishing tail. "Far out!" Jane laughed.

Grampa laughed too. "They call that <u>Oxtail</u> at the store. I'm 73 and I never seen an ox. It's just plain tail and it's the toughest part of all. But," he defended gallantly, "oxtail makes grand soup and stew. Cook it forever and it's real good eatin'." He added gloomily, "Don't cost much though."

He slapped the animal's rear. "Back here's the <u>Round Steak</u> and the <u>Rump Roasts</u>. Don't cost as much as the middle section 'cause they're tougher. So you have to cook 'em longer."

"This is all so meaningful," Jane trilled. "Tell us about the front part, the part near the front legs. What in the world do you call that?"

Grampa and Dick smiled at her high spirits. Grampa answered, "That's called <u>Chuck</u>. Chuck is medium tender, medium price, and you do most anything with it. Some folks broil a <u>Chuck Steak</u> just like a <u>Sirloin</u>."

The steer wandered off. Dick tugged at Grampa's elbow, shouting merrily, "Wicked! Can we go see the pigsty now? Can we?"

Since the fence was gone, sold to a collector, all three just skipped gaily over to the muddy spot behind the silo where the pigs lay. Grampa poked one in the tummy affectionately with his boot. He said, "There's a mint of money right there. <u>Bacon</u>. Yes, sir! Practically nothing but <u>fat</u>; just cooks to nothing right before your eyes. Folks buy it though."

Grampa pointed to the back legs. "The <u>Ham</u> is back here." He nodded with satisfaction. "I get a good price for that too, but" - he pointed - "you see how the front leg is smaller? That's the <u>Picnic</u> or <u>Cottage Ham</u>. Can't get too much cash for it." Grampa turned grumpily and started back to the house.

It was a big surprise to see the sunny open space where the barn had been. Grandma had just sold all the weathered sides to an architect. Her Gloria Vanderbilt jeans were bulging with cash.

Jane looked puzzled. "What bums me out is, all these pigs eat things like soybeans and cheap, simple grains. Bizarre! Why don't <u>we</u> eat seeds and soybeans too? It's the same protein and would be much cheaper, wouldn't it?"

Grampa eyed her suspiciously. "Maybe you kids better run along now. Like you say, buzz off."

"Good-bye, Grandma and Grampa," said Dick and Jane.

Grampa watched the disappearing Porsche. "Seeds! Beans! I hope those kids don't join one of them funny religions!"

Grandma didn't hear. She was busy as a bee selling the front door and a section of the porch railing.

++

SHOPPING

++

+ <u>ASK, AND IT SHALL BE GRANTED UNTO YOU . . .</u> +

YOU DON'T <u>have</u> to buy a pound package of chicken livers if you only want four of them. You don't <u>have</u> to accept a dozen oranges if you only want 2. You <u>can</u> ask the butcher to cut off just 1 rib of the big roast, or repackage the ground meat for a smaller quantity.

We have made all these embarrassing requests in dozens of stores and never found a refusal. Trained workers in good stores are there to help you. Maybe it even creates a diversion.

The only exceptions are when the prices apply to quantity buying - like a bunch of scallions, a sack of potatoes, or a bushel of something. But, generally, you can buy only as much as you want and select it personally and be choosy. Be pleasant, firm.

+ <u>SHOPPING CHECKLIST</u> +

This is just an elbow-nudger - a list of basics and staples that you can refer to before shopping. Add specific ingredients called for in each menu you plan to use. Take the book to the market.

+ <u>Dairy</u> +

Milk	Eggs
Butter or margarine	Cheese

+ <u>Seasonings</u> +

Salt	Dillweed
Pepper	Dijon mustard
Oregano	Paprika
Thyme	Worcestershire sauce
Basil	Ketchup
Tarragon	

+ <u>Produce</u> +

Onions	Potatoes
Garlic	Fruit, fruit, fruit

+ <u>Staples</u> +

Flour (stone-ground, preferably)	Bread
Sugar	Coffee
Salad oil	Tea
Vinegar, wine, or cider	Jelly or jam
Instant beef bouillon mix	Spaghetti
Instant chicken bouillon mix	Rice, Uncle Ben's converted
Mayonnaise, Hellmann's	

ANCIENT MAYAN SECRET REVEALED

HOW TO ADD POUNDS AND LOSE WEIGHT WITHOUT EXERCISE!

HOW TO ACQUIRE DEEP POWERS OF CONCENTRATION
AND TIGERLIKE REACTION TIME, SIMULTANEOUSLY,
WHILE SITTING DOWN!

HOW TO INCREASE CIRCULATION WHILE STAYING IN BED!

HOW TO REMAIN ACCIDENT-FREE ON A REGULAR BASIS!

EAT a good breakfast, daily.

Each day is an arena of contests. Dashing into it without good solid food in the body is a startling health risk. With no morning food you get low blood sugar, lose your quick reaction time and concentration. People who don't eat breakfast even have more accidents. And they'll probably gain weight; studies show they snack more all through the day.

If you don't eat breakfast, perhaps it's because you don't like the things usually served. Alone in your own kitchen you can eat your favorite foods: peanut butter, pickled herring, salami, cheese and crackers. Remember that most cooked food tastes even better the second day: right-from-the-refrigerator baked beans, cold pork, spaghetti, etc., can hit the spot, and quickly.

It's said the average American eats about 100 pounds of sugar per year. We're not spooning it out of the bowl, of course. Most of it is hidden in processed foods and a LOT is in commercial breakfast foods. Read labels. Ingredients are listed with those in largest proportions first. If the item you love lists sugar in the top three, think about it.

Be creative; make up your own breakfasts. Here are some of the more conventional breakfast foods and a few items you might never have heard of . . .

+ FRIED EGGS +

Put smallest, heaviest frying pan on medium heat for about 1 minute.

Crack 1 or 2 eggs smartly on the lip of a cup and drop them in.

Melt 1 tablespoon butter in the heated pan, to cover bottom. Add eggs, sprinkle with salt and pepper. Cover pan with a lid, to trap moisture. This process cooks bottom and steams top of eggs simultaneously. Peer at them in about a minute. The cloudier the top, the more "done" they will be.

+ SOFT-BOILED EGGS +

Make 1 piece of toast.

Put eggs in a saucepan, cover with cold tap water, place over high heat. Cover with lid. Set timer for 6 minutes or check your watch.

When cooked, drain off water, hold eggs under cold tap water for a few seconds, then crack them into a bowl or cup, scooping them out with a spoon. Add a teaspoon or more butter. Break up toast and add it. Add a little salt and pepper, mix all thoroughly.

This crisp-soggy little creation is delicious for breakfast, lunch, or at midnight.

+ BAKED EGGS +

Get dressed while these cook.

The minute you get up, turn the oven to 350. Melt 2 tablespoons butter in small, ovenproof skillet, on stove top. Swish around. Break in 2 eggs. Spoon some of the melted butter over the eggs, add salt and pepper.

Place in hot oven, uncovered. These will be ready when you're dressed, in 8 to 10 minutes, and you can eat them over the sink directly from the bubbling pan. No plate to wash.

In more patrician circumstances, they're called shirred eggs.

+ POACHED EGG +
(At last! The secret unleashed. How to poach a firm, nonraggedy egg.)

Put 2 inches water into small saucepan, heat water to a simmer (water surface is disturbed but not popping).

Put egg, in shell, in a cup of very hot tap water. Count slowly up to 20. (This will help tighten egg white.) Pour out the water.

Carefully open egg into cup.

Stir the simmering water 2 or 3 times viciously, creating a whirlpool. Slide the egg into the center of the water. Immediately remove pan from heat and cover it. Wait 4 minutes. Remove with slotted spoon. You have a poached egg.

Eat it on buttered toast.

+ COMMENT +

To make poached eggs in advance for several people (Brunch?): Cook one at a time, as above. Instantly put each egg into a sieve set in a bowl of cold water. To serve, immerse eggs in sieve in a saucepan of hot, but not boiling, water for about 30 seconds. There may be white streamers; they don't matter, but snipping with scissors is the best way to eliminate.

+ HARD-BOILED EGGS +

Put eggs in a saucepan, cover with cold water. (Cold water prevents unseen cracks from frothing over.) Cover pan, cook over medium heat for 15 minutes. Immediately pour off hot water. Add cold tap water to pan to cover eggs and stop the cooking. Mark eggs with a pencil for easy identification in the refrigerator.

+ OMELET WITH CHEESE FOR 1 PERSON +

This particular combination of bland cheese with the egg produces a delicate, almost poetic flavor and is also quite filling. We have gone to some length to describe the omelet, because the technique is so handy in using up leftovers. If feeding more than one, make each omelet individually because you can control the heat better, and because they're very satisfactory little exercises.

1 egg	3 strips cream cheese, little-finger size
1 or 2 tablespoons butter or	(my girlish finger)
margarine	1 finger Cheddar cheese

Heat 8″ skillet over medium heat. Put egg in small bowl and beat lightly with a fork for 20 seconds.

Melt butter in pan to coat bottom. When bubbling, add beaten egg and swirl it over butter. As it cooks, lift egg at edges, tilt pan, to let raw egg run under and cook.

In 30 seconds or so, scatter cheese on just one side of egg, near center. At once, put spatula under other side, at edge, and flip it to cover cheese. Let this cook for 10-15 seconds. If you feel deft, flip the whole thing over to brown the other side. Serve. No salt is needed here because of the cheeses.

+ COMMENT +

For a quick and filling supper dish, add any cooked meat or vegetables. Invent your own.

+ HOW TO COOK BACON +

The slices will cook more evenly if you cut them in half. Put in cold frying pan, cook over medium heat. Turn once. Drain on paper towel or brown-paper bag.

+ <u>HOW TO COOK SAUSAGE</u> +

Cook <u>bulk sausage</u>, in small patties, like bacon above.
<u>Sausage links</u> should be cut apart. Put them in a skillet with about ½ cup water.
Cover pan. Simmer sausages for 8 to 10 minutes (pork must be cooked well-done).
Remove cover, pour water off; or let it evaporate. Now cook sausages until brown. Drain
on paper towel.

+ <u>MILK TOAST</u> +

1 thick slice hot buttered toast   Brown sugar, maybe
1 cup <u>hot</u> milk

Put toast in heated shallow soup bowl. Pour milk over. Add sugar if you like. Serve hot.

+ <u>YOGURT CHEESE</u> +

The only peculiar thing about this is that you need a piece of <u>cheesecloth</u>
(supermarket or housewares store). Use <u>1 small size</u> (½ pint) <u>PLAIN yogurt</u> the first
time. You'll like the result - use a full pint next time. Line a mesh strainer with a couple
of layers of cheesecloth, put in yogurt, set strainer over a bowl. Leave in strainer
overnight. Don't refrigerate.
Next morning, <u>voilà</u>! Yogurt cheese. Refrigerate. It tastes a bit like cream cheese, but
with more zip. It's good on toast, with jam.

+ <u>INSTANT GAZPACHO</u> +

This is not only quick, it's cheap, nutritious, and possibly electrifying. You make it
with last night's leftover salad.
Put about <u>1 cup of good, cold salad</u> in a strainer. Drain at sink. Put salad into a
blender. Add ½ cup or more <u>V-8 or tomato juice</u>, a dash or two of <u>Worcestershire Sauce</u>,
drops of <u>Tabasco</u>. Blend for 5 or 10 seconds. Pour into a glass.

ON FREEZING & THAWING (page 17)
++++++++++++++++++++++++

+ <u>MONDAY</u> +

    Herb-Baked Chicken
    Boiled Potatoes
    Buttered Green Peas

+ <u>TUESDAY</u> +

    Crustless Quiche Easy-ola
    Tossed Green Salad with Diced Tomatoes
    Traditional French Dressing
    Garlic Bread

+ <u>WEDNESDAY</u> +

    Bunless Burgers
    Baked Potatoes
    String Beans in Herb Butter

+ <u>THURSDAY</u> +

    Spaghetti Marinara
    Spinach Salad with Plain Dressing
    Hot Italian Bread

+ <u>FRIDAY</u> +

    Easy Fish Parmesan
    Diced Creamed Potatoes
    Collard Greens

+ <u>SATURDAY</u> +

    Miracle Skillet Lasagna
    Herbed Bread
    Fruit

+ <u>SUNDAY</u> +

    All Saturday night main dishes are <u>extra</u> large.
    Make excellent leftovers.

    OR, make Brunch (page 84); invite a friend.

    The above applies 52 weeks a year, so we won't repeat it.

Please! Always read through all the recipes on the menu before you start.

+ +
MENU (serves 2)   Herb-Baked Chicken
                       Boiled Potatoes
                       Buttered Green Peas

+ +

+ HERB-BAKED CHICKEN +   Preparation: 10 minutes
                               Cooking: 50 minutes

A quick nonsplatter version of Southern fried chicken and no drive to the Colonel.

LINE UP YOUR INGREDIENTS:

2½- to 3-lb. chicken fryer, cut up   ½ teaspoon paprika
4 tablespoons butter or margarine   ½ teaspoon EACH basil, thyme, and
1 cup Bisquick   oregano
1 teaspoon salt   1 cup milk
Pepper to taste

PREPARATION:

Turn oven to 350. Close oven door.

Rinse your hands. Now, rinse chicken parts quickly under cold water. Pat dry with paper towels. Put aside innards (neck, gizzard, heart, liver) for later use. Remove excess yellow fat and discard, or melt for later use. See page 57.

In a 13″ × 9″ × 2″ shallow roasting pan, melt butter on stove over medium-low heat. Remove pan to counter.

In a medium-size paper bag measure the dry ingredients: the Bisquick, salt, pepper, paprika, and herbs. Shake bag.

Shake each piece of chicken in the bag till well coated with the floury mixture.

Place chicken, skin side down, in roasting pan. Spoon some melted butter onto each piece.

Place pan on center rack of oven. Close door. Cook 25 minutes.

Turn chicken pieces over. Bake 25 minutes more.

Turn off oven heat. Remove chicken from pan to platter and put it back into oven to keep warm, or cover with foil.

+ CREAM GRAVY +   Takes 6-7 minutes

Place roasting pan over medium heat on stove to heat up. Add 1 tablespoon of the above floury mixture.

Slowly add the milk, stirring with wire whisk to scrape all bits stuck to the bottom. Stir till gravy thickens, about 5 minutes. Taste with wooden spoon. If necessary, add ¼ teaspoon salt, and pepper, and stir again. Pour over chicken and serve.

+ COMMENTS +

1. Place the gizzard, heart, and neck in plastic baggie, tightly sealed, and freeze till you want to make Real Homemade Chicken Soup; see below.

2. You can save the leftover chicken bones and carcass for the same use. Adds to the soup's flavor.

3. REAL HOMEMADE CHICKEN SOUP: Takes 1 hour. In 2-quart saucepan put innards (neck, gizzard, heart), plus carcass and all old chewed-on bones. Peel and chop a large onion and 1 clove of garlic, 1 teaspoon basil or favorite herb, 2 sliced celery stalks plus leaves, some parsley, and add 3-4 cups water plus 1 teaspoon salt. Bring to boil over high heat. Turn to low. Cover. Simmer 1 hour. Drain through strainer into large bowl. Pick out any bits of neck meat or gizzard, etc. Cut up. Add back to soup. This keeps in refrigerator 3-4 days and can be used as soup with rice or noodles, or as "stock" as a base for sauces and gravies.

4. Freeze the precious liver. Then, sometime, try Hugo's Chicken Livers Supreme, on page 85. You'll need to collect and freeze about 4 livers in all.

5. Cooking with Chicken Fat Schmaltz: See page 57.

+ + + + + + + + + + +

+ BOILED POTATOES +   Cooking: 30-40 minutes

About the same calorie count as an equal-size apple, and full of vitamins B, C, iron, and other minerals, IF cooked unpeeled.

PREPARATION:

Cook 2 medium-size potatoes in enough boiling water to cover them.

After 30 minutes, test for doneness by stabbing one with a fork. If fork penetrates easily, they're cooked. If not, boil 10 minutes more. Drain at sink.

How to peel off hot potato skin and save your own: Spear a potato with kitchen fork. Hold aloft, and peel with a sharp knife. Or, holding potato in left hand, run it under cool tap water once or twice while quickly peeling. The jacket should slip off easily.

Return potato to saucepan. Keep covered with paper towel to absorb steam till dinner's ready.

Good plain, or with salt, pepper, and generous chunks of butter. Small boiled potatoes are good with skins left on.

+ + + + + + + + + + + +

+ BUTTERED GREEN PEAS +

Vegetable cooking does not involve sorcery. Simplicity is the key: Cook them in very little water, for a very short time, till just tender. Drain them promptly. Never let them sit in cooking water. They get soggy and lose color, vitamins, and flavor. It's good thinking to drink the cooking water, or save it for your soup pot, because that's where lots of precious nutrients are. So don't pour them away.

INGREDIENTS:

1 package frozen peas, or 1 can of peas	1 tablespoon butter Salt to taste

PREPARATION:

Cook peas when everything is done and ready.

If frozen peas, follow package instructions. But add the salt <u>after</u> cooking. (Salt extracts vitamins during cooking.)

If canned peas, plop them in a small skillet or saucepan. Heat through 2-3 minutes over medium heat. Drain. (Drink the juice later.) Return to skillet.

Add butter. Mix to melt and blend.

All daily meals are planned for 2.

+ + + + + + + + + + + + + + + + + + +

+ +

TUESDAY - First Week - TUESDAY - First Week - TUESDAY - First Week - TUESDAY -

+ +

+ +

MENU (serves 2):

        Crustless Quiche Easy-ola

        Tossed Green Salad with Diced Tomatoes

        Traditional French Dressing

        Garlic Bread

+ +

+ <u>CRUSTLESS QUICHE EASY-OLA</u> +   Preparation: 15 minutes
                                             Cooking: 25 minutes

Quiche, that delectable, creamy, pie-shaped French invention, is rapidly becoming a national passion. The flavor here is light and elusive, for the cauliflower seems to disappear in both taste and texture.

LINE UP YOUR INGREDIENTS:

Butter	½ cup Bisquick
1 package frozen cauliflower	3 eggs
1 small onion	½ teaspoon salt
1 large green pepper	¼ teaspoon pepper
4 oz. mild Cheddar cheese	1 cup milk

PREPARATION:

Grease a 9" pie pan with butter.
Boil cauliflower 10 minutes. (This is longer than package directions.) Drain it well, into sieve, over sink. Put cauliflower in pie pan.
Peel onion. Chop it up. (See page 16)
Mash cauliflower with fork until mushy. Spread it evenly on bottom of pie pan.
Turn oven to 350.
Cut green pepper in half. Remove seeds and stem. Chop up.
Grate cheese on large holes of grater.
Into a mixing bowl, in this order, measure in the Bisquick, eggs, salt, and pepper. Beat well, mixing thoroughly.
Add milk slowly, ¼ cup at a time, stirring enthusiastically after each addition. When you see no lumps, add the onion, green pepper, and cheese to the mixture. Stir to blend.
Pour from mixing bowl into pie pan.
Place pan on center rack of oven. Bake at 350 for 20-25 minutes, or till a thin knife, inserted into quiche center, comes out clean.
Remove to counter. Let it stand 5 minutes to set before cutting into portions.

+ <u>COMMENTS</u> +

1. Quiche (pronounced "key-shh") traditionally is a pie with a pie crust and is made of eggs, milk or cream, and cheese. Often bacon bits or ham is included. It is custardy and savory. There are other quiche recipes in this book; try them too.
2. This is an ideal BRUNCH dish. You can add more things. A good chance to be creative.

+ + + + + + + + + + + +

+ <u>TOSSED GREEN SALAD WITH DICED TOMATOES</u> +

Make before you tackle main dish. Then it's all ready, crisp and cold, to be served promptly.

INGREDIENTS:

6 large romaine or 12 Boston lettuce   1 medium tomato
    leaves

Wash lettuce in cold water. Dry with towel. Tear into bite-size pieces with fingers. Place in medium mixing (or salad) bowl. Refrigerate.

Cut up tomato into small pieces. Put in a cup. Refrigerate.

To serve, drain tomatoes, add to lettuce, pour on Traditional French Dressing. (Lettuce and tomato are kept separate so lettuce won't wilt in water from the tomato, which can also dilute your dressing.)

+ + + + + + + + + + +

+ TRADITIONAL FRENCH DRESSING +

Anything "traditional" follows a rule. This one's as simple as "3 to 1." That means 3 parts oil to 1 part vinegar. Since you use so little, use the best oil and vinegar for salads. Armed with these two rules, you'll never miss.

INGREDIENTS:

¼ teaspoon mild imported mustard   1 tablespoon red-wine vinegar (or cider
    (Dijon is best)   vinegar)
¼ teaspoon salt   3 tablespoons olive oil
⅛ teaspoon pepper   ½ teaspoon cold water

PREPARATION:

In small mixing bowl, dab in mustard. Add salt and pepper. Add vinegar. Stir. Pour in oil and water. Using a small whisk, or dinner fork, briskly stir together, blending well. Set aside to "age."

At serving time, stir well again. Pour over lettuce and tomatoes. Toss with 2 large spoons about 15 times (count aloud), or until leaves are well coated with dressing.

+ + + + + + + + + + + +

+ GARLIC BREAD +   Takes 20 minutes to warm

1 small loaf Italian bread (hero-size), or   1 large clove garlic
    one long loaf cut in thirds. Save   2 tablespoons butter or margarine
    two-thirds for midweek meals.   2 tablespoons oil (salad)

Cut bread in wide 2″ slices, but cut only ¾ of the way down through loaf, keeping bottom side intact. Place on a sheet of aluminum foil.

Peel and mash garlic.

In smallest skillet, melt butter and oil over medium heat. When melted, add garlic. Stir. Let it cook 30 seconds but don't let it brown. (Burnt garlic is bitter.)

Remove skillet to counter beside bread. Spread garlic-butter mixture evenly between slices. Encase bread in foil. Wrap tightly.

Put in oven beside quiche for 20 minutes.

To serve: UNWRAP. ("Foil, on plate, is unsightly as cigar in swimming pool" - old Chinese proverb.)

+ +

WEDNESDAY - First Week - WEDNESDAY - First Week - WEDNESDAY - First Week -

+ +

Read through EVERYTHING, once over lightly!

+ +
MENU (serves 2):   Bunless Burgers
                      Baked Potatoes
                      String Beans in Herb Butter
+ +

+ BUNLESS BURGERS +   Preparation: 15 minutes
                                       Cooking: 15 minutes

These luscious hamburgers are round, German style, instead of flat, so they turn out crispy brown outside, pink and juicy within.

LINE UP YOUR INGREDIENTS:

½ lb. ground beef   3 tablespoons butter or margarine
2 medium-size onions   Salt and pepper

PREPARATION:

Rinse your hands. Leave them wet, but not dripping. (Makes it easier to shape the meat.)
Make four rounded hamburgers. Set them aside.
Now, wash and dry your hands.
Peel and slice onions.
Melt butter in 12" skillet over medium heat.
Add sliced onions. Fry, stirring now and then, for about 5 minutes, or until onions are limp and golden, but don't let them burn. (Burnt onions taste bitterish.)
Remove onions to a plate with slotted spoon.
Put hamburger balls into skillet. Brown on all sides over medium-high heat.
Turn heat down a bit, to medium, and cook hamburgers, turning once or twice. This takes 8-10 minutes.

Return onions to skillet. Dust all lightly with salt and pepper. Stir around once or twice. Serve the burgers smothered with onions. Delicious!

+ COMMENTS +

1. Plain hamburgers, flattened, are cooked the same way, using just a little butter and less cooking time, about 5 minutes rare, 7-8 minutes for medium.
2. To peel onion quickly: Immerse in a bowl of very hot tap water for 1-2 minutes.

+ + + + + + + + + +

+ BAKED POTATOES +   Takes 1 to 1½ hours

WATCH THIS! The potatoes require the longest cooking time. So, start them far ahead of everything else. Waiting is worth it, for these vitamin-rich, buttery wonders. (Idaho potatoes are best for baking.)

Turn oven to 425 to preheat. Keep door of oven tightly closed. Wash 2 Idaho potatoes. Scrub them clean. Dry thoroughly. Moisten skins by rubbing with a dab of oil. Place on center rack of oven. Bake at 425 for an hour.

Test for doneness: Use a potholder to grab a potato. Squeeze gently. If done, it feels tender and gives to the squeeze. If hard and resistant, it's not ready; bake up to 30 minutes more. Remove from oven, turn OFF oven. Prick skins once or twice to let steam escape. Return to oven to keep warm till entire dinner's cooked.

To serve: Cut a long slit lengthwise and a short slit across it forming a cross. Squeeze potato open. Imbed a large chunk of butter in each potato.

+ COMMENTS +

1. In some restaurants, potatoes are baked wrapped in foil and brought thusly to the table. No! "Foil on a plate is as unappetizing as a hairbrush in the refrigerator" - old Irish potato proverb.
2. Don't throw the skins away. Make a "Skin Sandwich." Put a big glop of butter in the middle, fold over, and enjoy it.

+ + + + + + + + + + +

+ STRING BEANS IN HERB BUTTER +   Takes 10 minutes

Anyone can cook plain string beans. These have class.

INGREDIENTS:

10-oz. package frozen string beans (or ½   ½ teaspoon dillweed (not "-seed")
     lb. fresh)   ¼ teaspoon salt
2 tablespoons butter or margarine

PREPARATION:

In small saucepan, cook frozen string beans according to package directions. (<u>Fresh beans</u>: Remove ends. Use 1 cup of water. Cover. Cook 8 minutes or till tender, and drain.)
Drain beans into strainer.
In saucepan, melt butter over medium heat. Add dill and salt. Stir a minute. Return beans to saucepan and stir to coat beans with herb butter. Serve.

+ +

THURSDAY - First Week - **THURSDAY** - First Week - **THURSDAY** - First Week -

+ +

+ + + + + + + + + + + + + + + + + + + +

MENU (serves 2): Spaghetti Marinara
                 Spinach Salad with Plain Dressing
                 Hot Italian Bread

+ +

+ <u>SPAGHETTI MARINARA</u> +   Preparation: 5 minutes
                                     Cooking: 35 minutes

Bravissimo! If you asked for "spaghetti with red sauce" in Italy, this is what you would get. It is authentic, delicate, and unlike any available commercially, so don't expect a thick gummy sauce which lies in an inert puddle on top; this sauce integrates with the pasta.

LINE UP YOUR INGREDIENTS:

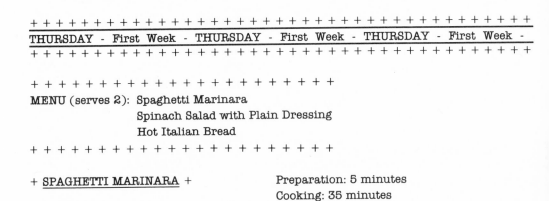

2 tablespoons olive oil

2-lb. can peeled tomatoes

2 teaspoons dried oregano

¼ bunch parsley (fresh), chopped

2 large cloves garlic, chopped

½ lb. thin spaghetti (or whichever you prefer)

1 tablespoon butter

2-3 tablespoons grated Parmesan cheese

PREPARATION:

In large saucepan bring oil to hot 1 minute over high heat. Add tomatoes and juice. Break up tomatoes, add oregano, parsley and garlic. Cover.
Turn down to medium-low. Cook for 30 minutes; stir now and then.
Meanwhile, in largest pot, bring water to boil over high heat. When it's a rolling boil, add spaghetti. Stir with a fork a few times to prevent spaghetti from sticking together. NO lid. Boil 8 minutes, or according to package directions.
Drain spaghetti into colander over sink.
Put in large bowl. Add a lump of butter. Pour sauce over it. Mix well.
Sprinkle grated cheese on top.

+ <u>COMMENTS</u> +

1. Any size or shape of pasta is fine here. (Try crazy shapes. The different textures actually change the flavor!) But remember, the thicker the spaghetti, the longer the boiling time. So read the box directions!

2. The more garlic you use, the better it tastes. One guy uses 17 cloves. He reports great results.

3. If you put a teaspoon of oil in the boiling spaghetti water <u>or</u> leave a long-handled wooden spoon in the pot, the water will not boil over.

+ + + + + + + + + + +

+ <u>SPINACH SALAD WITH PLAIN DRESSING</u> +   Takes 10 minutes

No flavor or vitamins are lost when you eat vegetables raw. Make this <u>before</u> you start dinner.

INGREDIENTS:

8 oz. fresh spinach (or ½ bag)   1 tablespoon wine vinegar
4 tablespoons olive oil   ¼ teaspoon salt

Before you start dinner, wash spinach well (unless it's prewashed in a bag) and remove thick stems. Dry well in towel. Tear into bite-size pieces. Refrigerate in bowl till dinner's ready.

Then, remove spinach from refrigerator and casually pour over it the oil, vinegar, and salt. Use two large spoons and toss salad 15 times. Perfection!

(There's another <u>spinach salad</u> in SUMMER SESSION that you should try sometime. It's wonderful.)

+ + + + + + + + + + +

+ <u>HOT ITALIAN BREAD</u> +

Use ⅓ of this week's long Italian loaf, or another hero-size loaf. Slice and toast. Use lots of butter. (<u>Sweet butter</u> is excellent with tonight's dinner. Also, try <u>whole-wheat</u> Italian bread.)

+ +
+ +

READ through all directions, <u>now</u>!

+ +
MENU (serves 2):   Easy Fish Parmesan
                          Diced Creamed Potatoes
                          Collard Greens
+ +

+ EASY FISH PARMESAN +

Preparation: 3 minutes
Cooking: 20 minutes

This recipe is birdbrain simple. It's made with fillets of flounder, but any fillets of a similar fish will substitute well and be equally tasty. So, let cost be your guide. Since thin fillets perform best here, some suggested fish to use are perch, fluke, sole, whiting, turbot, or pollack.

LINE UP YOUR INGREDIENTS:

4 tablespoons butter or margarine
  (½ stick)
2 oz. (½ cup) grated Parmesan or
  Romano cheese

4 fillets of flounder (fresh or frozen; see COMMENTS), about ¾ lb.

PREPARATION:

Turn oven to 400. Close door.

Slice butter and melt in small saucepan over medium heat. Don't let it brown. Pour HALF the butter into an ovenproof 9″ × 9″ square cake pan or similar-size pan.

Sprinkle half the grated cheese on the butter, evenly. Lay the fish fillets on top of the cheese. Pour other HALF of melted butter on the fish. Dust the top of the fish with remaining cheese.

Place pan on center rack of oven. Bake 10 minutes.

Remove pan. Close oven door to keep heat inside.

With largest spoon, scoop up juices alongside fish fillets and baste over the top. Return pan to oven.

Bake 10 minutes more. (Add 5 minutes additional baking time if fillets are thicker than ½ inch.) Serve immediately.

+ COMMENTS +

1. Fish fillets cook faster than whole fish.
2. Fish fillets are more expensive than whole fish, BUT . . .
3. Fish fillets have no waste.
4. Fillets are perfect for people in a hurry.
5. Fillets are perfect for people who hate bones.

+ TO DEFROST FROZEN FISH +

1. Unwrap. Leave on counter on a plate, or in sink, 2 hours, OR . . .
2. Unwrap. Rewrap WELL in plastic. Submerge in cold water for 20-30 minutes, OR . . .
3. Remove from freezer. Leave in lower refrigerator section OVERNIGHT.
4. When fish is defrosted, dry well with paper towel before using. This matters especially if you want to fry the fish.

+ <u>DICED CREAMED POTATOES</u> +   Takes 15 minutes

These potatoes are a snap. They take half the cooking time of whole potatoes, and the taste is smooth and old-fashioned. Start them <u>before</u> cooking the fish.

LINE UP YOUR INGREDIENTS:

2 medium potatoes   2 tablespoons butter
¼ cup milk   ½ teaspoon salt

PREPARATION:

Peel potatoes. Rinse them under cold water, then cut into dice. (To do this: Halve potatoes, lengthwise. Place flat, cut side down. Cut into ½" slices. Then, cut across at ½" intervals.)
Place diced potatoes in a saucepan. Add enough water to cover.
Bring to boil over high heat. Turn heat to low. Cover pan. Simmer for 10 minutes.
Drain into sieve over sink. Return potatoes to saucepan.
Add milk, butter, and salt. Bring to a boil over high heat. Stir to bottom to prevent scorching. Quickly, turn DOWN heat to medium. Cook at a gentle bubble 3-4 minutes, till most, BUT NOT ALL, liquid has boiled away. Stir often.
Remove from heat. Cover. Let sit till fish is done.

+ + + + + + + + + + + +

+ <u>COLLARD GREENS</u> +   Preparation: 10 minutes
                                               Cooking: 35 minutes

Crammed with vitamins and obscure minerals, collards are the greens of the South and have produced many fine athletes.

LINE UP YOUR INGREDIENTS:

1 lb. fresh collards, or 1 package frozen   3 strips bacon
        (see COMMENTS)   Salt and pepper

PREPARATION:

In sink full of cold water, immerse fresh collards and swish around. Remove. Shake water off.
Trim off any roots. Slice across in narrow strips.

Cut up bacon into 1″ widths. Fry in 12″ skillet for 2-3 minutes, till some fat melts into pan, over medium heat.

Add cut-up collards, cover <u>tightly</u>. Cook on low heat 25-30 minutes. Stir well. Pepper. Maybe salt. Serve.

+ <u>COMMENTS</u> +

If you use frozen collards, just put them right on top of the half-fried bacon, and cover pan tightly. After 10 minutes or so, break up and separate collards with wooden spoon. Cover. Cook on low 30 minutes.

+ +
SATURDAY - First Week - SATURDAY - First Week - SATURDAY - First Week - SATURDAY
+ +

LAST REMINDER: Read through all the recipes first!

+ + + + + + + + + + + + + + + + + + + +
MENU (serves 2 — for 2 days!):
>Miracle Skillet Lasagna
>Herbed Italian Bread
>Fruit
+ + + + + + + + + + + + + + + + + + + +

+ <u>MIRACLE SKILLET LASAGNA</u> +   Preparation: 10 minutes
Cooking: 45 minutes

Most lasagna needs 4 hands, 5 pots, and half the day. This recipe produces a spicy dish that's lighter, better tasting, and made in just 1 pan throughout.

LINE UP YOUR INGREDIENTS:

2 tablespoons butter
1 lb. ground beef
1 envelope spaghetti sauce mix
1 lb. creamy cottage cheese
3 cups broad egg noodles, uncooked
Parsley (fresh)
2 teaspoons basil

1 teaspoon salt, optional
1 cup water
1-lb. can tomatoes
8-oz. can tomato sauce
8 oz. mozzarella cheese, shredded or in
>thin slices

PREPARATION:

In large 12″ skillet, melt butter over medium heat. Add beef and stir around till all pink disappears. Remove pan from stove to counter.

Sprinkle on HALF the spaghetti sauce mix, and stir in well.

Spoon cottage cheese over top of beef, evenly. Scatter dry noodles all over cheese.

With scissors, snip up parsley fine, about 2 tablespoons. Sprinkle parsley and basil evenly over everything.

Over all, pour the tomatoes plus juice, the rest of the tomato sauce, salt, and the cup of water. (Break solid tomatoes into pieces with knife or fingers.) Make sure all is moistened throughout.

Return skillet to stove. Bring to bubbling on <u>high</u> heat. QUICKLY turn heat down to <u>low</u>. Cover. Simmer for 35 minutes.

Remove skillet from stove. Uncover. Top with mozzarella. Cover again. Let stand 5 minutes, or till cheese melts.

+ <u>COMMENTS</u> +

1. There's enough here to last through 2 days of meals, which means you can relax! Refrigerate, covered, in an oven casserole.

2. To reheat, simply cover and let it warm through in 350 oven about 15 minutes.

+ + + + + + + + + + +

+ <u>HERBED ITALIAN BREAD</u> +

This is a quickie spin-off of garlic bread; fast because it's run under the broiler for a matter of seconds.

INGREDIENTS:

⅓ loaf Italian bread, or hero-size loaf	½ teaspoon basil
2 tablespoons butter or margarine	½ teaspoon oregano

Before dinner is ready, do this: Split bread lengthwise. On a saucer or flat dish, mash butter, basil, and oregano together. (Use a dinner fork.) Spread bread halves with herb butter. Put in cake pan, butter side up. Set aside for later.

When dinner's ready: Turn oven to broil. Place rack about 7″ from heat. Put cake pan with bread on center of rack. Watch closely. In 15-30 seconds the bread will be bubbly and brown. Remove and serve.

+ + + + + + + + + + +

MENUS for SECOND WEEK

+ <u>MONDAY</u> +

    Braised Italian Chicken Hugo
    Fluffy White Rice
    Fresh Buttered Spinach

+ <u>TUESDAY</u> +

    Fake Cheese Soufflé
    Chinese Broccoli
    Bean Sprout Salad

+ <u>WEDNESDAY</u> +

    Middle East Meatballs in Yogurt Sauce
    Bulgur Wheat Pilaf
    String Bean Salad with Italian Dressing

+ <u>THURSDAY</u> +

    Fettucini
    Tomato-Watercress Salad with Italian Dressing

+ <u>FRIDAY</u> +

    Salmon Loaf, Creamy Sauce with Crunch
    Chunky Browned Potatoes
    Tri-Colored Salad

+ <u>SATURDAY</u> +

    Russian Roast Pork with Sour-Cream Gravy
    Kasha
    Brussels Sprouts, hot or cold

+ +
MENU (serves 2):   Braised Italian Chicken Hugo
                    Fluffy White Rice
                    Fresh Buttered Spinach
+ +

+ BRAISED ITALIAN CHICKEN HUGO +   Preparation: 10 minutes
                                    Cooking: 45 minutes

The chicken turns out golden brown, the vegetables mostly disappear to make a light gravy, and your kitchen wafts forth irresistible aromas - same effect as walking into a fine Italian restaurant.

LINE UP YOUR INGREDIENTS:

2½- to 3-lb. chicken fryer, cut up
2 strips bacon
4 mushrooms
1 green pepper
3 large cloves of garlic
2 tablespoons parsley

½ teaspoon EACH of basil, oregano, thyme
Salt and pepper
¼ lemon, or 2 tablespoons lemon juice
2 tablespoons olive oil (optional)

PREPARATION:

Remove any excess lumps of yellow chicken fat and discard, or use as described on page 57.

Cut up bacon into 1" pieces. Distribute evenly over bottom of large 12" skillet. On top of bacon place the chicken, skin side down.

Turn heat to high. When bacon starts sputtering, turn heat to medium-high and begin to brown the chicken. Turn the chicken pieces over 2-3 times during browning. The whole process should take about 15 minutes.

Meantime, while browning, prepare the vegetables:

Wipe and slice mushrooms - tops and stems.

Cut open green pepper. Remove seeds and stem. Slice.

Peel and chop up garlic. Snip up parsley.

When chicken is nicely browned all over, add the vegetables and lemon juice. Give everything a little stir around so vegetables will drop to bottom of pan. Sprinkle in herbs. (Add 2 tablespoons of olive oil if you have it on hand.)

Turn heat to low. Cover tightly - cook 15 minutes. Turn chicken pieces. Cover tightly again. Cook 15 more minutes.

Serve on a bed of fluffy rice.

Use the pan gravy to pour over chicken and rice.

+ <u>COMMENTS</u> +

In this one, you can brown and cook the innards (neck, gizzard, heart, and liver) along with the chicken. Or, you might want to reserve the liver and freeze it along with last week's piece till you have enough to make <u>Hugo's Chicken Livers Supreme</u>, page 85.

+ + + + + + + + + + +

+ <u>FLUFFY WHITE RICE</u> +   Takes 20-25 minutes

Certain dishes just beg for rice. This is one of them. Please remember most rice is cooked 2 to 1, which means twice as much water as rice. Exception is brown rice, which needs a bit more water.

INGREDIENTS:

1½ cups water   ¾ cup Uncle Ben's converted rice
1 teaspoon salt   1 tablespoon butter or margarine

PREPARATION:

Bring water to a boil. Add salt and rice. Stir to separate rice. Turn heat to low. Cover pan. Simmer 20 minutes, or till all water is absorbed. Add butter. Stir and serve, or keep warm by covering (off heat) till dinner's ready.

+ <u>COMMENT</u> +

Uncle Ben's rice is specified because it's nutritionally best of the white rices. Unpolished is good too, but hard to find. "Minute" rice tastes like soaked minced cardboard.

+ + + + + + + + + + +

+ <u>FRESH BUTTERED SPINACH</u> +   12 minutes, total

Something easy to do with that leftover ½ bag of fresh spinach from last week. It also works with a <u>defrosted</u> package of frozen chopped spinach.

INGREDIENTS:

½ bag (8 oz.) fresh spinach (or 10 oz.   2 tablespoons butter or oil
    frozen chopped, <u>defrosted</u>)   ¼ teaspoon salt

PREPARATION:

Wash and dry spinach. Remove stems. Slice leaves thin on a wooden surface.

(If using defrosted spinach, squeeze it _dry_ with hands or between 2 dinner plates, over sink.)

In 8" skillet, melt butter over medium heat. When it's bubbly, add spinach. Cook, stirring often, for 2-3 minutes. Spinach should be limp but not a sodden mass. Sprinkle in salt. Stir to mix. Serve immediately.

+ +

TUESDAY - Second Week - TUESDAY - Second Week - TUESDAY - Second Week - TUESDAY

+ +

+ +
MENU (serves 2):   Fake Cheese Soufflé
                        Chinese Broccoli
                        Bean Sprout Salad
+ +

+ FAKE CHEESE SOUFFLÉ +   Preparation: 15 minutes
                                 Cooking: 45 minutes

Sometimes called "strata," this is freestyle layers of bread, cheese, herbs which are then drowned in an egg sauce to produce a sort-of soufflé. Tastes 100% better than it sounds and heated leftovers are just as good.

LINE UP YOUR INGREDIENTS:

6 slices white or whole-wheat bread,   4 eggs
    crusts removed (regular slice, not   4 tablespoons butter
    thin)   2 cups (1 pint) half-and-half cream
½ lb. Cheddar cheese, shredded   2-3 dashes Tabasco
½ teaspoon salt   1 teaspoon Worcestershire sauce
½ teaspoon basil   ½ teaspoon Dijon mustard
1 teaspoon oregano

PREPARATION:

Grease a 9" × 5" loaf pan or a 2-quart casserole dish.
Break bread into bite-size bits.
Shred cheese on large holes of grater.

Line bottom of pan with HALF of the bread pieces.

Cover bread with HALF the shredded cheese.

Over this, evenly sprinkle salt and herbs.

Scatter remainder of bread for next layer.

Reserve 3 tablespoons of cheese; layer the rest on the bread.

Now turn oven to 350, and make SAUCE:

SAUCE:

In a large mixing bowl, beat eggs.

In a small skillet melt butter. Set aside to cool.

To mixing bowl add cream, Tabasco, Worcestershire sauce, and mustard. Mix well. Now, add melted butter. Stir to blend.

Pour contents of bowl into bread-cheese pan. Make sure this sauce dampens all contents. Top with remaining cheese. Do not cover.

Bake at 350, on center rack of oven, for 45 minutes. Let rest on counter for 10 minutes to set before serving. Scoop onto plates, using large spoon.

+ COMMENTS +

1. Try this first as written. For variations: Before you pour in the sauce, you might try adding a cup of any leftover vegetables, i.e., peas, carrots, corn, limas, sliced zucchini. Chopped spinach is wonderful. Or a chopped tomato - excellent. Also, a medium-size onion - for zing.

2. Meat eaters: Throw in any leftover cut-up COOKED meat, poultry, or seafood. Bacon and ham are especially good.

3. BUTSY'S SIMPLIFIED SAUCE: Delicious and goes like this: 2 eggs beaten into 1 can of cream of mushroom or celery soup, 1½ cups milk, 2 tablespoons melted butter, all mixed together and poured over the layers of bread-and-cheese.

+ + + + + + + + + + +

+ CHINESE BROCCOLI +   Takes 10 minutes

A cooking method borrowed from the Chinese. This will be delicious hot, lukewarm, or cold.

LINE UP YOUR INGREDIENTS:

1 package frozen broccoli stems (not chopped)

2 large cloves of garlic

2 tablespoons peanut or vegetable oil

½ teaspoon salt

PREPARATION:

Put broccoli in saucepan with water according to package instructions. Bring to boil over high heat. Separate stems gently with fork. Cover, cook till barely tender, 4-5 minutes.

Drain into sieve over sink. Dry on paper towels to remove excess water. Set aside.

Peel and mash, or finely cut up, the garlic.

In skillet, heat oil and salt over high heat. (Takes about 1 minute.) Turn down heat to medium. Add garlic. Let it sizzle, but not brown.

Quickly toss in the cooked broccoli. Stir fast in the hot oil for 2 minutes. Remove from heat. Put on a plate till ready to serve. (If it remains in pan, it will get limp and lose its charm.)

+ COMMENT +

Store-label frozen vegetables are as good as the brand names and cheaper. AVOID the preflavored buttered kind in a pouch. These are super-expensive and a nuisance to handle.

+ + + + + + + + + + +

+ BEAN SPROUT SALAD +

Especially for those who don't eat meat, bean sprouts are a necessity - a total-food nutritional booster. (Soybeans are top of that list.) Equally good raw or cooked. You'll find other bean-sprout recipes in POST GRADUATE section. Make this salad before cooking dinner.

INGREDIENTS:

10-oz. bag fresh bean sprouts (or 14-oz. can)	1 large clove garlic
	1 tablespoon wine vinegar
¼ teaspoon salt	4 tablespoons olive oil

PREPARATION:

Remove long, thin ends of sprouts and discard. (If using canned: Drain bean sprouts into strainer. Rinse with cold water. Shake dry.)

In mixing bowl, put salt. Peel and cut up garlic. Add it to salt. Use back of a wooden spoon to mash the garlic well into the salt.

Add vinegar and oil. Mix well with whisk or dinner fork. Add bean sprouts. Stir, and toss 15 times. Refrigerate till dinner is served.

+ COMMENT +

This salad can be made more colorful by adding 2 sliced scallions (white and greens), some thin sliced red radishes, and some fine slivers of green pepper. Adding 1 tablespoon soy sauce is a nice Chinese touch.

+ +
WEDNESDAY - Second Week - WEDNESDAY - Second Week - WEDNESDAY - Second Week
+ +

+ + + + + + + + + + + + + + + + + + +
MENU (serves 2):
    Middle East Meatballs in Yogurt Sauce
    Bulgur Wheat Pilaf
    String Bean Salad with Italian Dressing
+ + + + + + + + + + + + + + + + + + +

| + MIDDLE EAST MEATBALLS IN YOGURT SAUCE + | Preparation: 15 minutes
Frying: 10 minutes
Baking: 30 minutes |

The best meatball recipe east or west of Baghdad, this instantly turns you into a 55-minute gourmet. It keeps well, refrigerated, for another meal and also takes kindly to freezing and reheating.

LINE UP YOUR INGREDIENTS:

1 egg
1 lb. ground chuck
¼ cup bread crumbs (or 1 slice white
    bread, crumbled fine)
1 teaspoon basil, thyme, or favorite herb

½ teaspoon salt
¼ cup plain yogurt (4 tablespoons)
2 scallions, or one small onion
3 tablespoons flour
3 tablespoons vegetable oil

SAUCE INGREDIENTS:

1 tablespoon butter
1 tablespoon flour
1 teaspoon paprika

½ cup chicken broth (made with ½ cup
    hot water and ½ teaspoon instant
    chicken bouillon mix)
¾ cup yogurt (i.e., what's now left of ½
    pint carton)

PREPARATION:

In mixing bowl, beat egg lightly with a fork. Add ground chuck, bread crumbs, basil, salt, and ¼ cup of the yogurt.

Remove root end of scallions, and chop up white and most of green parts too. Add to bowl.

Rinse hands - leave them damp. Mix all in bowl well, with hands. (Very professional.)

Form 18-20 golfball-size meatballs and put them on a CLEAN counter space.

Put flour on large dinner plate. Roll half the meatballs in it.

Heat oil in a 12″ skillet over medium-high heat. Add meat balls.

Fry 2-3 minutes till brown. Turn them with slotted spoon. Fry 2-3 minutes more. With slotted spoon, remove meatballs to a nearby bowl or plate.

Roll remaining balls in flour and fry them in the hot oil, as you did the others.

When all the balls are brown, pour off fat from the skillet into grease can, rinse pan quickly under cold water, and dry well.

Turn oven to 350. While it's heating, make your SAUCE.

SAUCE:

In same skillet melt butter over medium heat. Add flour and paprika. Stir quickly. Remove from heat.

Melt ½ teaspoon chicken bouillon in ½ cup hot water. Add slowly to skillet, stirring.

Return skillet to heat. Stir 3 minutes till thickened. REMOVE FROM HEAT.

Add yogurt. Stir well.

Add meatballs. Stir to cover gently with sauce. Cover pan. Put in oven on center rack. Bake 30 minutes at 350.

+ COMMENTS +

Heat separates yogurt so your sauce may have grainy appearance. It will taste just fine.

Tomorrow, reheated, the sauce will appear grainier. Not to worry; the flavor is still great.

+ + + + + + + + + + +

+ BULGUR WHEAT PILAF +   Takes 20 minutes

Serves 2 for 2 days. Cheap, delicious, filling.

LINE UP YOUR INGREDIENTS:

1 medium onion
2 tablespoons butter
½ cup bulgur wheat
1 teaspoon chicken bouillon mix

1 cup boiling water
Salt
2 tablespoons parsley

PREPARATION:

Peel and chop the onion. Melt the butter in a medium-size saucepan over medium-high heat. Add the onion. Cook 3 minutes. Stir frequently.

Add the bulgur wheat. Stir to mix thoroughly with onion.

Add the chicken broth (1 teaspoon melted in the 1 cup boiling water) and about ½ teaspoon of salt.

Bring to a boil over high heat. Turn to low. Cover. Simmer 15 minutes.

Snip up parsley with scissors or chop well. Stir into wheat. Serve while steaming hot.

+ + + + + + + + + + + +

+ STRING BEAN SALAD WITH ITALIAN DRESSING +

Do this ahead of time, before starting dinner. It really needs to get itself together for a while by resting in its dressing. (The term is "marinating.") Drain a <u>can of whole string beans</u>. Put them in a small mixing bowl. Pour <u>Italian Dressing</u> over them. Refrigerate till dinner.

+ COMMENT +

This can also be made with cooked fresh, or frozen, string beans. <u>Much</u> better, but more work.

+ ITALIAN DRESSING +

¼ teaspoon salt
⅛ teaspoon pepper
1 clove garlic

1 tablespoon wine vinegar
½ teaspoon cold water
3 tablespoons olive, or salad, oil

In mixing bowl, put salt and pepper. Peel and slice garlic into bowl. With back of a wooden spoon, mash garlic firmly into salt till it's a pulpy mass. (A garlic press would do same thing in a flash.)

Add vinegar and water and stir. Add oil and beat with a whisk or dinner fork till well mixed. Pour over string beans. Mix gently. Refrigerate.

HOW TO CLEAN UP (page 15)
+++++++++++++++++++

+ + + + + + + + + + + + + + + + + + +
MENU (serves 2):   Fettucini
                         Tomato-Watercress Salad
                           with Italian Dressing
+ + + + + + + + + + + + + + + + + + +

+ FETTUCINI +

Preparation: 5 minutes
Cooking: 8 minutes

Although "fettucini" merely means "flat, thin noodles," this special combination of ingredients is of such ancient lineage and fame that fettucini just means this one beloved recipe to most people. (Maybe you've heard of Fettucini Alfredo? Same thing. There are multiple Alfredos from Rome to Hong Kong who say they have a corner on the original.) Note the quick preparation and cooking times. This should be served AT ONCE.

LINE UP YOUR INGREDIENTS:

Salt
½ lb. linguine or thin, FLAT pasta or
     noodles
1 stick soft butter

½ cup grated Romano or Parmesan
     cheese (fresh-grated if you want to
     be another Alfredo)
¾ cup light cream

PREPARATION:

In largest pot bring 3 quarts of water to a boil. Add 1 tablespoon salt.
Add linguine. Stir a bit till water boils again, so that the pasta won't stick together in gummed-up lumps.
Boil according to box directions for timing.
When cooked tender, yet firm (NOT mushy), drain into LARGE sieve or colander over sink.
Put in large bowl. Cut in butter. Mix well and quickly.
Add cheese and cream. Mix again fast. Serve immediately.

+ + + + + + + + + + + +

+ TOMATO-WATERCRESS SALAD WITH ITALIAN DRESSING +

Watercress is easier to handle and even better for you than most salad greens. Besides that, its unique, zippy flavor and lovely dark-green color make it the real gourmet's preference. Use 1 bunch of watercress and cut off long stems. Discard; better, munch while cooking dinner. Cut the whole bunch into 3 sections crosswise and put in a mixing bowl. Cut 1 medium tomato into bite-size pieces; drain. Add to bowl. Make Italian Dressing, page 48. Pour it over salad. Mix well. Serve.

+ <u>COMMENT</u> +

Sorry about this: Check price of watercress. Can be priced out of sight at times. Buy only
when gorgeous (i.e., in season and cheapest).

+ +

FRIDAY - Second Week - FRIDAY - Second Week - FRIDAY - Second Week - FRIDAY - Second

+ +

+ + + + + + + + + + + + + + + + + + + +
MENU (serves 2):   Salmon Loaf
                  Creamy Sauce with Crunch
                  Chunky Browned Potatoes
                  Tri-Colored Salad
+ + + + + + + + + + + + + + + + + + + +

+ <u>SALMON LOAF</u> +   Preparation: 15 minutes
                           Cooking: 45 minutes

Remember cafeteria salmon? You'll be happy to hear this isn't it. The loaf is airy, herb-
flavored, with a delightful sauce you may even want to double next time.

LINE UP YOUR INGREDIENTS:

1 egg
1-lb. can salmon (red or pink)
⅔ cup light cream
3-4 slices bread, crumbled
Handful minced parsley (about ½
     bunch)

1 small onion
½ teaspoon salt
½ teaspoon basil
3 dashes of Tabasco (optional)
Butter or oil

SAUCE:

2 tablespoons butter
2 tablespoons flour
1 cup milk
¼ cup mayonnaise (4 tablespoons)

¼ cup chopped olives (smallest can; or
     chop pitted olives yourself)
¼ cup chopped nuts (any kind except
     peanuts), optional

PREPARATION:

Preheat oven to 350.

In large bowl, beat egg with whisk till yellow. Whisk in cream.

Open salmon. Dump salmon and juice into beaten egg. Mash with fork (center bone is edible).

Make bread crumbs. Add to bowl. Snip parsley with scissors. Add to bowl. Add salt, basil, 2-3 dashes of Tabasco. Peel and chop onion. Add onion and cream.

Mix and bash everything together well.

Grease bread loaf pan with a little butter or oil. Spoon salmon mixture into loaf pan evenly. Smooth top but don't pack tight.

Bake on center rack of oven 45 minutes, or till center is firm. (Test firmness: Slip a thin knife into center. If it comes out clean, loaf is done.)

While loaf bakes, make the Creamy Sauce with Crunch.

+ CREAMY SAUCE WITH CRUNCH +

Over medium heat, in saucepan, melt butter. Add flour, stir briskly 30 seconds. Remove from heat.

SLOWLY add milk, bit by bit, stirring after each addition so no lumps form. Return pan to heat. Cook, stirring gently, 3-4 minutes or till sauce thickens.

Remove from heat. Add mayonnaise. Stir. Drain chopped olives. Add olives and chopped nuts to sauce. Stir well. Cover.

When loaf is cooked, reheat sauce 1-2 minutes on medium-low. Spoon it over each slice of loaf.

+ + + + + + + + + + + +

+ CHUNKY BROWNED POTATOES +   Takes 15 minutes

Simple. Fast. Buttery delicious. A perfect accompaniment to the salmon-loaf main course and many others.

LINE UP YOUR INGREDIENTS:

2 tablespoons chopped parsley	2 tablespoons vegetable oil
2 medium-size potatoes	Salt and pepper
2 tablespoons butter or margarine	

PREPARATION:

With scissors, snip up parsley fine. (Much easier than chopping.) Set it aside on a saucer.

Pare potatoes. Rinse under cold water. Cut potatoes into small chunks, about ½" cubes.

Place in saucepan with just enough water to cover. Bring to a boil over <u>high</u> heat. Turn heat down to low. Cover pan. Simmer 10 minutes.

Drain into sieve over sink. Turn potatoes onto a towel; dry well.

Melt butter and oil together in a small skillet over medium-high heat. When bubbly hot, dump potatoes into pan. Sprinkle in a little salt and pepper. Toss the potatoes continually with a spatula till they're crumbly. Then toss frequently till they turn golden.

Throw in parsley. Turn once or twice, and serve soon.

+ + + + + + + + + + +

+ <u>TRI-COLORED SALAD</u> +

Cheery, gay mixture - mostly out of cans.

INGREDIENTS:

8-oz. can whole string beans	1 tablespoon vinegar (or lemon juice)
8-oz. can sliced beets	½ teaspoon salt
2-3 scallions	¼ teaspoon pepper
3 tablespoons olive oil	

PREPARATION:

Drain string beans and beets. Put them in a mixing bowl.

Remove root ends of scallions. Slice scallions lengthwise, then cut up fine crosswise. Add to bowl.

Add olive oil, vinegar, salt, pepper. Mix thoroughly. Refrigerate till dinner is ready.

+ +
SATURDAY - Second Week - SATURDAY - Second Week - SATURDAY - Second Week - SAT
+ +

+ + + + + + + + + + + + + + + + + + + +
MENU (serves 2 for 2 days!):
      Russian Roast Pork with Sour-Cream Gravy
      Kasha
      Brussels Sprouts, hot or cold
+ +

+ RUSSIAN ROAST PORK
WITH SOUR-CREAM GRAVY +

Preparation: 10 minutes
Waiting: 15 minutes
Roasting: 2 hours

The facts are: Pork needs long, slow cooking; pork is often reasonable in price; this pork is tender, flavorful, moist; sandwiches made of cold pork are a treat.

LINE UP YOUR INGREDIENTS:

2-3 lb. pork loin roast, boned
4 mushrooms
2 tablespoons lemon juice (½ fresh
    lemon)

2 cups chicken stock (2 teaspoons
    instant chicken bouillon mix in 2
    cups hot water)
Salt and pepper
½ cup (4 oz.) sour cream

PREPARATION:

Using a thin-bladed knife, you will be making slits in the pork, about 1-2" deep and 1" wide. Then you'll insert sliced mushrooms in the slits. Do it this way:

Slice mushrooms fairly thin.

Make a slit; leave knife in and tilt a bit. Insert a slice in slit; pull out knife, holding down mushroom slice. Make another slit. Insert another slice. And so on until all slices are used up.

Put pork in small roasting pan or iron skillet. Rub pork all over with 2 tablespoons lemon juice, dribbling a lot of it into the slits if possible. Lightly salt and pepper the roast on all sides.

Let sit in pan for 15 minutes, marinating. Meanwhile, turn oven to 450.

When oven is hot, put roast on center rack. Let brown for 20 minutes.

Turn oven DOWN to 350. Pour chicken stock over roast. Roast for 2 hours.

Every half hour, open oven and, with long-handled spoon, baste pan juices all over pork. This assures moistness of meat.

When done, remove from oven to platter.

With big spoon, skim off clear excess fat in pan to a grease jar (old coffee can).

Blend sour cream into remaining pan juices till fairly well mixed. Spoon over roast. Divine!

+ COMMENT +

The mushrooms in the slits release moisture which makes the pork tender and juicy.

+ + + + + + + + + + + +

+ KASHA +

Takes 30 minutes in all

Also called buckwheat groats, this vitamin-rich grain has a nutty wheat flavor that makes kasha a perfect accompaniment for pork, duck, and lamb kabobs. Slavic in origin, it is rapidly becoming a part of our scene.

LINE UP YOUR INGREDIENTS:

1 egg
1 cup kasha
1 large onion
1 large clove garlic

2 tablespoons butter, margarine, or
     rendered Chicken Fat (page 57)
2 cups water
½ teaspoon salt

PREPARATION:

In mixing bowl: Beat egg. Add kasha. Mix well.
Peel and chop up onion and garlic.
In 2-quart saucepan: Melt butter over medium heat. Add onion and garlic. Cook, stirring a bit, till onions are limp (3-4 minutes).
Add kasha mixture. Stir and fry till kasha forms separated grains, looks like uncooked rice (about 2 minutes).
Add water and salt. Stir to bottom. Turn heat to <u>high</u>. Bring to a boil.
Quickly turn heat to <u>low</u>. Cover pan. Simmer 20 minutes, or till liquid is absorbed and kasha is tender. (Add more salt if necessary.)

+ + + + + + + + + + +

+ BRUSSELS SPROUTS +

What to say? Either you like 'em or you don't. If you don't, chances are you've never had them fresh enough and cooked properly. Good sprouts are sweet as candy. (Overcooking is the prime crime, making them soggy and sour. Minimum cooking is the key.) Check price. Usually cheap.
Choose ½ lb. smallest brussels sprouts (or 10-oz. package frozen). Trim ends off fresh sprouts, and wash. Put in saucepan with water barely to cover. Bring to a boil. Boil 2 minutes. Turn heat to medium. Cook, covered, 5-7 minutes. (Test with fork for doneness. If it slips into sprout easily, they're cooked.) Drain at sink, turn back into pan. Add ¼ teaspoon salt and 2 tablespoons butter or oil. Mix well. Serve immediately. Don't let them languish in the pot.

+ COMMENTS +

For a nice change, try BUD'S COLD MARINATED BRUSSELS SPROUTS: Cook sprouts as above. Drain at sink. Put them in a bowl, add about ¼ cup Italian dressing of your own make, or a supermarket bottled one with no sweet taste.
Refrigerate sprouts several hours or overnight. Some people keep these in a jar in the refrigerator as an always-there appetizer.

+ + + + + + + + + + +

+ <u>MONDAY</u> +

    Chicken Tarragon Sauté
    Buttered Noodles
    Zucchini Southern Style

+ <u>TUESDAY</u> +

    Spinach Pie
    Chick-Pea Salad
    Fruit

+ <u>WEDNESDAY</u> +

    Survival #2 Beef Casserole
    Icy Sliced Cucumbers

+ <u>THURSDAY</u> +

    Macaroni and Cheese Primavera
    Buttered Chopped Broccoli

+ <u>FRIDAY</u> +

    Ruthie's Louisiana Fish Creole
    Rice Pilaf
    Corn Niblets

+ <u>SATURDAY</u> +

    Peasant Meat Loaf
    Carrot-Turnip Combo
    Iceberg Lettuce with Russian Dressing

+ + + + + + + + + + + + + + + + + + + +
MENU (serves 2):   Chicken Tarragon Sauté
                          Buttered Noodles
                          Zucchini Southern Style
+ + + + + + + + + + + + + + + + + + + +

+ CHICKEN TARRAGON SAUTÉ +   Preparation: 5 minutes
                                    Cooking: 40 minutes

This very quick French method of cooking produces extremely tender chicken. It has an elusive flavor and a gorgeous color.

LINE UP YOUR INGREDIENTS:

2½-lb. chicken fryer, cut up   2 thick scallions
Salt and pepper   ½ cup chicken broth (made with ½
2 tablespoons butter   teaspoon instant chicken bouillon
1 tablespoon oil   mix and ½ cup hot water)
1 teaspoon tarragon

PREPARATION:

Cooking chicken by this method produces the most tender, juicy chicken in the world. It also produces an amount of splattering that is unavoidable. If you own a splatter shield (large, round MESH thing, long-handled) use as a lid here; helps contain splatters. Clean up later with paper toweling.

Wash your hands. Now wash the chicken, rinsing quickly under cold-water tap. Pat DRY with paper towels.

Lightly salt and pepper both sides of chicken pieces. Remove any large bits of excess yellow chicken fat. Discard, or save for later use; see page 57.

If the chicken legs and thighs are still connected, use a sharp knife and make a deep cut halfway through the joint bones, or sever them altogether. (Makes the chicken cook through more thoroughly.)

Use 12″ skillet. Get it warm over medium heat. Melt butter. When bubbly, add chicken pieces, skin side down. Sauté 20 minutes till deep golden-brown color. Shake pan now and then so chicken doesn't stick to bottom.

Turn chicken pieces. Sprinkle HALF the tarragon into the butter. Sauté chicken 20 minutes more.

Remove chicken to large plate or platter. Pour grease out of skillet into a cup.

Remove root end of scallions. Slice scallions lengthwise, then cut them up in thin slivers crosswise. Add scallions and other HALF of tarragon to skillet. Return 1 tablespoon of grease from cup to skillet.

Cook, stirring, 1 minute over medium heat.

Pour in chicken broth. Cook and scrape the bottom of skillet with wooden spoon to swirl all collected bits into broth. Let bubble 1-2 minutes.

Pour all over chicken.

+ COMMENTS +

1. Wrap chicken liver in plastic bag and freeze till you collect enough livers to make Hugo's Chicken Livers Supreme (see page 85).

2. CHICKEN FAT (Schmaltz): Cut up chicken fat into bits. Chop a small onion. Fry both in smallest skillet over medium heat till fat is completely melted (rendered). Strain fat into little jar or can. Refrigerate. Use later, instead of butter, for frying. (Makes potatoes taste divine.)

3. Save neck, gizzards, heart, chewed-on bones, and carcass to make REAL HOMEMADE Chicken Soup (see page 28).

+ + + + + + + + + + +

+ BUTTERED NOODLES +   Takes 10 minutes

Buy 8-oz. package medium-broad egg noodles. Cook in large pot according to package directions. Drain into strainer at sink. Return to pot. Add 1-2 tablespoons butter or margarine, salt, and pepper, and stir well to melt and mix.

+ + + + + + + + + + +

+ ZUCCHINI SOUTHERN STYLE +   Preparation: 10 minutes
                                   Cooking: 20 minutes

You have never, repeat never, tasted zucchini done better. An old southern recipe from an old friend.

LINE UP YOUR INGREDIENTS:

2-3 medium zucchini (about ¾ lb.)   1 medium onion
2 slices bacon   Salt and pepper

PREPARATION:

Wash zucchini well under cold tap water. Cut off ends. Slice 1" thick. Put aside.

Cut up bacon in 1" pieces. Put in 2-quart saucepan.

Peel and chop onion. Put in saucepan. Add zucchini.

Cover pan. Put on medium heat. Cook 15-20 minutes. Stir around 2-3 times during cooking.

Add salt and pepper to taste. Serve.

+ + + + + + + + + + + + + + + + + + + +

MENU (serves 2): 　　　　　Spinach Pie
　　　　　　　　　　　　　Chick-Pea Salad
　　　　　　　　　　　　　Fruit

+ + + + + + + + + + + + + + + + + + + +

+ SPINACH PIE + 　　　　　　　　　Preparation: 15 minutes
　　　　　　　　　　　　　　　　Cooking: 45 minutes

This is a grand quiche. Two people can make a meal of it. In narrow wedges, it's a perfect party appetizer. You can serve it as a side dish to take the place of vegetables and potatoes. The never-fail method lets you rely on it for any emergency. Keep the ingredients on hand.

LINE UP YOUR INGREDIENTS:

9" frozen unbaked pie shell (Mrs. Smith's is excellent)
1 package frozen chopped spinach
3 eggs (2 eggs plus 1 yolk)
¼ cup light cream or half-and-half

1 can cream of mushroom soup
4-oz. can sliced mushrooms, drained
1 small onion
1 garlic clove
¼ teaspoon salt

PREPARATION:

Turn oven to 350. Defrost piecrust for 10 minutes, on counter top.

MEANWHILE:

Boil spinach according to package instructions. Drain into strainer over sink. (For EASIEST way to extract spinach moisture, place spinach between two dinner plates. Hold over sink and squeeze plates together. Spinach is now bone dry.)

In large bowl, with a fork, beat eggs and yolk.

Add spinach, cream, soup, and drained mushrooms.

Peel and chop onion and mash garlic. Add to bowl. Mix thoroughly. Pour into piecrust.

Place pie on bottom rack of oven. Bake at 350 for 30-40 minutes, or until a knife inserted gently comes out clean.

Let set on counter 5 minutes before serving.

+ + + + + + + + + + + +

+ CHICK-PEA SALAD +

There's nothing to this, but its simplicity belies its terrific flavor. A favorite legume (see dictionary on legumes) in Mexico, South America, and among most Spanish-speaking peoples, chick-peas (garbanzos) add a generous helping of protein to the meal. Make this salad <u>before</u> you start the meal.

Open a <u>can of garbanzos</u> (chick-peas). Drain at sink. Put in large mixing or salad bowl. Thinly slice <u>½ small head iceberg lettuce</u> and add to bowl. In a small bowl, put <u>½ teaspoon salt</u> and <u>1 clove of garlic</u>, peeled and cut up. Use back of a wooden spoon to mash garlic and incorporate it with salt. Add <u>4 tablespoons olive oil</u> and <u>1 tablespoon lemon juice</u>. Mix well. Pour over salad. Stir and mix. Refrigerate until dinner.

+ +
+ +

+ +
MENU (serves 2):   Survival #2 Beef Casserole
                Icy Sliced Cucumbers
+ +

+ <u>SURVIVAL #2 BEEF CASSEROLE</u> +   Preparation: 30 minutes
                                 Cooking: 20 minutes

A one-pot complete dinner here, which reheats well and freezes too. The Italian sausage adds a spicy flavor.

LINE UP YOUR INGREDIENTS:

1 large onion
1 large clove garlic
½ lb. sweet Italian sausages (4 links)
½ lb. ground beef
½ cup rice
1½ cups water
1½ teaspoons instant chicken bouillon
    mix

10-oz. package frozen Italian green
    beans, or cut string beans
1 teaspoon oregano
1 teaspoon basil
½ teaspoon thyme
Salt
4- to 6-oz. package sliced or shredded
    provolone cheese

PREPARATION:

Peel and chop up onion and garlic. Set aside.

In large 12″ skillet, brown sausage meat. (If you've bought sausage links, simply squeeze the meat out of casings, using fingers.) Fry sausage meat 3-4 minutes over medium-high heat, breaking up into bits with wooden spoon as it cooks.

Add beef. Break up and stir now and then. Fry till pink of the meat disappears.

Add onion and garlic. Cook 3-4 minutes. Stir and scrape skillet bottom now and then to prevent sticking.

Add rice, water, instant bouillon mix, frozen beans, oregano, basil, thyme, and about ½ teaspoon salt. Stir around till beans separate.

Turn heat to <u>high</u>. Bring to boil. Quickly cover. Turn to <u>low</u>. Cook, bubbling gently, 20 minutes.

Uncover, top with cheese. Re-cover. Cook 2-3 minutes, till cheese is melty.

+ COMMENT +

Do not store food in refrigerator in iron skillet.

+ + + + + + + + + + + +

+ ICY SLICED CUCUMBERS +

<u>Important</u>! Make this before starting dinner.

Peel, remove ends, and thinly slice (paper thin) <u>1 large cucumber</u>. Put in a bowl. Add <u>1 teaspoon salt</u>. Mix well. Refrigerate. At dinnertime: Drain cucumber slices into sieve at sink. Return to bowl. Mix in <u>2 tablespoons olive oil</u>. Add more salt if too bland. Serve <u>now</u>.

+ COMMENTS +

1. If you hate seeds: Slice cucumber in half lengthwise. Run a teaspoon down centers to scoop out seeds.

2. If you find cucumbers in the market whose skins have <u>not</u> been oiled, or waxed, you don't need to peel them.

3. To flute (prettify) cucumbers: Remove ends; peel. Run a dinner fork down the length of cuke, all the way around it. When you then slice it thin, slices will have attractive, professional-looking edges.

+ +
+ +

+ + + + + + + + + + + + + + + + + + + +
MENU (serves 2): Macaroni and Cheese Primavera
              Buttered Chopped Broccoli
+ + + + + + + + + + + + + + + + + + + +

+ MACARONI AND CHEESE PRIMAVERA +

Preparation: 10 minutes
Cooking: 20 minutes

"Primavera" means spring. Here's the old warhorse Macaroni and Cheese gussied up with some vegetable surprises for taste and vitamins.

LINE UP YOUR INGREDIENTS:

1½ cups elbow macaroni	½ teaspoon salt
2 small zucchini (½ lb.)	1 teaspoon basil
3 scallions	2 tablespoons flour
2 tablespoons butter	1 cup milk
8-oz. can tomatoes	4 oz. mild Cheddar cheese, shredded

PREPARATION:

In 2-quart saucepan, bring 3 cups water to a boil. Add macaroni. Cook at a rolling boil till barely tender, about 7 minutes. Don't cover.

Drain into sieve at sink. Set aside, in saucepan.

While macaroni is cooking, wash zucchini well in cold water and dry off with paper towel. Remove ends. Slice thinly, ¼ inch.

Remove root end of scallions. Slice crosswise, using the white part and most of the green stems.

In 12" skillet, melt butter on medium heat. Add zucchini and scallions. Cook 4 minutes. Stir a bit.

Add tomatoes with the juice, salt, and basil. Break up tomatoes with a fork. Cook on medium heat 5 minutes.

Sprinkle in flour. Stir around till flour disappears. Add the milk. Stir till mixture thickens, 3-4 minutes.

Add Primavera sauce to the cooked macaroni in saucepan; add shredded cheese. Stir a bit. Cover; cook on low heat 5 minutes.

+ + + + + + + + + + + +

+ BUTTERED CHOPPED BROCCOLI +

Takes 10 minutes

INGREDIENTS:

10-oz. package frozen chopped broccoli	¼ teaspoon salt
1 small (4-oz.) can sliced mushrooms (optional)	1 tablespoon butter

Cook broccoli according to package instructions. Drain at sink into strainer.

In small saucepan, heat mushrooms in their juice over high heat, 1 minute. Drain. Add to broccoli. Return to saucepan. Add salt and butter. Stir to melt. Serve.

+ + + + + + + + + + + + + + + + + + + +
MENU (serves 2):   Ruthie's Louisiana Fish Creole
                   Rice Pilaf
                   Corn Niblets
+ +

+ RUTHIE'S LOUISIANA FISH CREOLE +   Preparation: 15 minutes
                                     Cooking: 35 minutes

The word "Creole" usually means the dish is part French, part Spanish. It is usually spicy, as is this.

LINE UP YOUR INGREDIENTS:

2 green peppers   ¼ teaspoon salt
1 medium onion   2-3 dashes of Tabasco
6 cloves garlic (yes, 6)   8-oz. can tomato sauce
5 mushrooms   1 tablespoon ketchup
2 tablespoons cooking oil (Wesson,   1 lb. boned fish (cod, halibut, monkfish,
     Mazola)   rockfish, haddock)

PREPARATION:

Remove seeds and stem of green pepper; chop up.
Peel and chop onion and garlic.
Wipe and slice mushrooms (caps and stems).
In 2-quart saucepan, warm oil over medium-high heat. Add green pepper, onion, mushrooms, and garlic. Stir frequently for 5 minutes, till vegetables are limp but not brown.
Add salt, Tabasco, tomato sauce, and ketchup.
Cover. Cook, on medium-low heat, 25 minutes.
Meanwhile: Cut up fish in large, bite-size pieces.
Uncover pan. Add fish. Re-cover. Cook 5 minutes more on medium heat. Serve over rice.

+ COMMENTS +

1. To remove skin of garlic easily: For 30 seconds immerse garlic cloves in very hot water. The skins will slip right off.
2. Want to try a fine MANHATTAN-STYLE (red) FISH CHOWDER? Use this recipe: Omit rice. Add an 8-oz. bottle of clam juice at the same time that you add the tomato sauce, etc., and cook on as recipe directs. Super.

+ + + + + + + + + + + +

Today's students are more sophisticated. They will eat fish.

+++

+ RICE PILAF +

Preparation: 5 minutes
Cooking: 20 minutes

Good enough to eat straight from saucepan, rice done this way gives you a home-style taste of the exotic Orient. It's firm and chewy, with a nutlike flavor.

INGREDIENTS:

½ cup Uncle Ben's converted rice
2 tablespoons butter or margarine or oil

1 medium onion
1 can Campbell's consommé

PREPARATION:

Peel and chop up onion. Melt butter in 8″ skillet over medium heat. Add onion. Cook, stirring a bit, 3 minutes.

Add rice. Stir till well coated (1 minute). Add consommé. Bring to a boil over <u>high</u> heat. Turn heat to <u>low</u>. Cover. Simmer 20 minutes. Serve.

+ + + + + + + + + + +

+ CORN NIBLETS +

Open an <u>8-oz. can of corn niblets</u>; pour into a small saucepan. Cook over high heat, in the juice, till they come to a boil and are heated through. Drain into strainer at sink.

Return niblets to saucepan. Add a <u>tablespoon of butter</u>. Stir and serve.

+ + + + + + + + + + + + + + + + + + + +
MENU (serves 2):

        Peasant Meat Loaf

        Carrot-Turnip Combo

        Iceberg Lettuce with Russian Dressing

+ +

+ <u>PEASANT MEAT LOAF</u> +   Preparation: 15 minutes

                                      Cooking: 1 hour

Country-style, simple and satisfying. Cold meat-loaf sandwiches tomorrow will taste good with ketchup.

LINE UP YOUR INGREDIENTS:

2 medium potatoes   1 large onion
2 eggs   ½ bunch parsley
1½ lb. ground beef   Ketchup, Worcestershire sauce,
1 teaspoon salt   mustard (optional)
½ teaspoon pepper

PREPARATION:

Turn oven to 350.

Peel potatoes and cut into ½-inch dice. Put in small saucepan with water to cover. Bring to boil. Cook 10 minutes. Drain into sieve over sink.

In mixing bowl, beat eggs a bit.

Add potatoes, meat, salt, and pepper to eggs. Peel and chop onion. Add to bowl. Rinse parsley under cold-water tap. Shake dry. Chop or snip parsley with scissors and add.

Rinse your hands. Mix ingredients in bowl with your hands till everything's distributed uniformly. Grease a loaf pan. Put mixture in it. Tap down gently. Smooth 2 tablespoons ketchup all over top.

Place pan on center rack of oven. Bake at 350 for 1 hour.

Remove from oven. Let set on counter 5 minutes before slicing. Put fork against meat to hold it in pan and carefully pour off excess fat which has accumulated on pan bottom. (Use an empty can for the melted fat. Hot fat and grease clog up sink drains.)

SAUCE (optional):

Combine (in small bowl) 2 tablespoons ketchup with 2 teaspoons Worcestershire sauce; OR 2 tablespoons ketchup with 2 teaspoons prepared mustard. Mix. This makes a nice sauce to spread lightly over meat-loaf slices.

+ COMMENTS +

Just as good tomorrow, Sunday night - sliced, reheated on medium-low heat in covered skillet for 5 minutes. Or use cold as a sandwich (pita bread) filler.

+ + + + + + + + + + +

+ CARROT-TURNIP COMBO +   Preparation: 5 minutes
                                 Cooking: 10 minutes

No way can this excellent combination be described. If you're apathetic about root vegetables, maybe a promise will help you plunge. It's delicious. A promise!

INGREDIENTS:

2 medium carrots   ½ teaspoon salt
2 small turnips (white)   3 tablespoons butter or margarine
½ bunch parsley

PREPARATION:

Scrape carrots. Cut in ½" slices.
Peel turnips. Cut in half. Place flat side down on wooden surface. Makes ½" slices. Then cut across in ½" slices; turnip falls into ½" dice.
Put carrots and turnips in saucepan with cold water to cover. Bring to a boil over high heat. Turn to low. Cover. Simmer 10 minutes.
Meanwhile, wash parsley. Shake dry. Remove stems and discard. Chop up parsley fine.
Drain vegetables in sieve at sink. Return to saucepan. Add salt, butter, parsley. Stir to mix. Cover to keep warm till ready to serve.

+ + + + + + + + + + +

+ ICEBERG LETTUCE WITH RUSSIAN DRESSING +

Make the dressing ahead of the meal-cooking. In small bowl mix: ½ cup Heinz ketchup, ½ cup Hellmann's mayonnaise, and ½ teaspoon Worcestershire sauce. Refrigerate till dinner.
Dinner time: Slice ½ small head of iceberg lettuce in thin slivers onto plates. Pour dressing on top of each serving. That's it.

+ + + + + + + + + + +

+ <u>MONDAY</u> +

Marie's Chicken Paprika in Yogurt Sauce
Brown Rice
Oven-Fried Eggplant Slices

+ <u>TUESDAY</u> +

Broccoli Chowder Andy
Toasted Pita Bread
Fruit

+ <u>WEDNESDAY</u> +

Barbecued Pork Ribs
Mashed Potatoes
Creamy Coleslaw

+ <u>THURSDAY</u> +

Marie's Eggplant Casserole
Lentils
Hot French Bread

+ <u>FRIDAY</u> +

Dilled Fish in Foil
Home-fried Potatoes
Tossed Green Salad with Diced Tomatoes (page 30)
Traditional French Dressing (page 31)

+ <u>SATURDAY</u> +

Baked Cottage Ham Butt
Southern-Style Cabbage
Easy Corn Fritters

+ +
MENU (serves 2):

      Marie's Chicken Paprika in Yogurt Sauce

      Brown Rice

      Oven-Fried Eggplant Slices

+ +

+ MARIE'S CHICKEN PAPRIKA IN YOGURT SAUCE +

Preparation: 5 minutes
Cooking: 45 minutes

You can zip through the preparation here in champion time. When it's done, it has a rosy paprika glow.

LINE UP YOUR INGREDIENTS:

8-oz. carton plain yogurt
2½- to 3-lb. chicken fryer, cut up
¼ cup flour
2 tablespoons vegetable oil
½ cup dry sherry, vermouth, or cider

½ cup chicken broth (made with ½
    teaspoon instant chicken bouillon
    mix dissolved in ½ cup hot water)
2 teaspoons paprika
½ teaspoon salt

PREPARATION:

Take yogurt out of refrigerator and bring to room temperature. Leave it open on counter top till later.

Wash chicken pieces and dry on paper towel. Put flour on a large plate. Dip pieces into it on both sides.

Heat oil in a 12″ skillet on medium-high. Add chicken. Brown 5 minutes on each side. Remove chicken to a plate.

Add sherry to skillet, and stir around to remove bits of chicken from pan bottom. Let cook 1 minute. (This is called "deglazing" the pan.) Add the chicken broth and 1 teaspoon of paprika.

Sprinkle chicken with 1 teaspoon more of paprika and put it in the skillet, skin side up. Use a large spoon to baste pan juices over the chicken. Sprinkle on salt.

Cover pan. Cook on medium-low 15 minutes. Uncover. Turn chicken pieces over. Cover. Cook 15 minutes more.

Remove chicken to a platter. Remove pan from heat. Swirl yogurt into pan. Stir a moment. Pour over chicken.

+ BROWN RICE +

Takes 45 minutes

Very different from regular white rice in flavor and texture. This type is grainier, more robust in taste. Recently it has gained favor with "natural-food" enthusiasts. With this main dish it is a natural.

Cook according to package instructions. Use ¾ cup natural brown rice to 2 cups water. When cooked, add 1 tablespoon butter and ½ teaspoon salt. Mix well. Cover till dinner is ready.

+ COMMENT +

Start this before you begin cooking dinner. It takes quite a while and it can wait.

+ + + + + + + + + + +

+ OVEN-FRIED EGGPLANT SLICES +   Preparation: 10 minutes
                                        Cooking: 12-15 minutes

In the Near East they say a person who can fry eggplant must be wealthy because this vegetable absorbs more than its weight of oil. Not with this method, however. And, you can prepare it in advance, bake it just before serving.

INGREDIENTS:

1 lb. eggplant (that's small)   ½ cup Parmesan or Romano cheese, grated
½ cup bread crumbs or cracker crumbs   1 cup Hellmann's mayonnaise

PREPARATION:

Peel eggplant. Remove stem end and top. Cut eggplant into ¼" to ½" slices.

Mix bread crumbs with grated cheese. Put on flat plate.

Put mayonnaise in cereal bowl.

Preheat oven to 400.

Dip each slice of eggplant into mayonnaise, covering edges, too. Next dip slices into bread crumb mixture, coating thoroughly all over. Place slices on a cookie sheet or on your 13" × 9" × 2" roasting pan.

Place pan on center rack of oven. Bake at 400 for 12-15 minutes, or till eggplant is golden brown.

Remove, with spatula, onto plates.

+ +
MENU (serves 2):   Broccoli Chowder Andy
                          Toasted Pita Bread
                          Fruit
+ +

+ <u>BROCCOLI CHOWDER ANDY</u> +   Preparation: 5 minutes
                                          Cooking: 15 minutes

A rough-textured, Swiss-style cheese soup. Jack said, "I never thought I'd like this, but I do." (Jack hates broccoli.)

LINE UP YOUR INGREDIENTS:

2 boxes frozen chopped broccoli
3 cups chicken broth (3 cups <u>hot</u> water
    plus 3 teaspoons instant chicken
    bouillon mix)
4 tablespoons butter or margarine

1 cup milk
1 teaspoon salt
1 cup light cream or half-and-half
2 cups (8 oz.) shredded Swiss cheese

PREPARATION:

Use a 3-quart saucepan. Cook broccoli in chicken broth 8 minutes, according to package instructions. <u>Do not drain</u>.
Add everything else to pot. Stir over low heat, 3-4 minutes. EAT!

+ <u>COMMENTS</u> +

1. If <u>fresh</u> broccoli is in season, and is cheap, you'll need 1½ to 2 lbs. Chop it up. Cook till fork-tender, about 10 minutes. Don't use the lower, woody parts of the stem. Too tough.
2. The cheese will melt a bit lumpy. That's OK. After all, it's a chowder, not a cream soup.

+ + + + + + + + + + + +

+ <u>TOASTED PITA BREAD</u> +

Split <u>3-4 pitas</u> open. Spread the insides with <u>butter</u>. Put them on a cookie sheet or in roasting pan, buttered side up. Turn oven to "broil." Brown them under the broiler LESS than 1 minute.

+ + + + + + + + + + + +

People who don't eat breakfast
have more accidents (page 22).
+++++++++++++++++++

+ + + + + + + + + + + + + + + + + + + +
MENU (serves 2):   Barbecued Pork Ribs
                            Mashed Potatoes
                            Creamy Coleslaw
+ + + + + + + + + + + + + + + + + + + +

+ <u>BARBECUED PORK RIBS</u> +   Preparation: 5 minutes
                                  Cooking: 2 hours

The sauce is a pungent, glistening lava which envelops the tender meat. Even the <u>bones</u> will be delicious and chewy. Long cooking time here, of course, because it's pork. The sauce has many other uses; see COMMENTS.

LINE UP YOUR INGREDIENTS:

2-3 lbs. thick "country-style" pork ribs   2 garlic cloves, mashed
1 package onion-soup mix   1 tablespoon oregano
1 cup ketchup   1 teaspoon Worcestershire sauce
1½ cups water

PREPARATION:

Turn oven to 325.
Line a 9″ × 9″ square cake tin, or similar-size pan, with aluminum foil to avoid messy clean-up later.
Peel and mash garlic in a mixing bowl. Add everything, <u>except</u> pork ribs, and stir.
Put pork ribs in pan. Pour barbecue sauce over them. Be sure lots gets on top.

Put in oven on center rack. Bake at 325 for 2 hours. Baste 2-3 times or more during baking period.

+ COMMENTS +

1. You can do BARBECUED PORK CHOPS or BARBECUED PORK LOIN exactly the same way, baking for the same amount of time. Use 4 thick center-cut chops for the first suggestion. Use a 2½- to 3½-lb. pork loin for the second. (These are meals for 4.)

2. SWORDFISH baked with this sauce is super. The oven baking time is only 30 minutes, but the sauce should be gently cooked 5 minutes extra in a saucepan before it is poured over fish in baking pan. (One lb. fish for 2 is plenty.)

3. This sauce works well on SHORT RIBS OF BEEF too. Same method: 325 oven for 1½ to 2 hours. (Buy meaty, thick ribs about 2" thick, 3" long. Not necessarily cheap, but terrific meat. Watch for specials at the market; odd cuts like this are quite often marked down.)

+ + + + + + + + + + +

+ MASHED POTATOES +   Takes 30 minutes

If you only had a potato ricer, you could make mashed potatoes? True. But you can do without. You work a little harder, but you still get what you want:

INGREDIENTS:

3 medium (tennis-ball size) potatoes	½ teaspoon salt
3 tablespoons butter or margarine	⅓ cup milk or light cream

PREPARATION:

Peel potatoes. Cut into 1" cubes. Put in 2-quart saucepan with cold water to cover. Bring to boil over high heat. Turn to medium low. Cover. Simmer for 20 minutes or till potatoes fall apart when you prod them with a fork. Drain at sink into strainer. Return to saucepan.

Add butter and salt. Bash around with wooden spoon. Switch to a dinner fork and mash some more. Slowly add milk, a bit at a time. Keep mashing with fork. (Don't use all the milk if mixture looks runny; use more milk (or cream) if it stays too stiff.) Switch to wooden spoon again and bash and whip around till all lumps disappear. Phew! Actually, because the potatoes were cut up, this is not all that hard to do.

Cover to keep warm.

+ + + + + + + + + + + +

+ CREAMY COLESLAW +   Takes 10 minutes

Make this before you start cooking dinner. Or get it into the refrigerator at least 1 hour ahead.

INGREDIENTS:

½ small (1 lb.) head green cabbage   ½ cup Hellmann's mayonnaise
1 medium carrot   ½ teaspoon salt
½ cup sour cream

PREPARATION:

As thin as possible, slice cabbage. Don't use core (discard). If slices are too long, cut in half. Put cabbage in large bowl.

Scrape carrot. Using vegetable peeler, slice into thin strips. Cut strips up a bit. (You don't want long strings of carrot.) Add to bowl.

Add sour cream, mayonnaise, salt. Mix very thoroughly. Refrigerate till dinner. Serve.

+ COMMENT +

If you have a grater, grate cabbage and carrot on large-hole side.

+ +
THURSDAY - Fourth Week - THURSDAY - Fourth Week - THURSDAY - Fourth Week -
+ +

+ + + + + + + + + + + + + + + + + + + +
MENU   (serves 2   Marie's Eggplant Casserole
       or more):   Lentils
                       Hot French Bread
+ +

+ MARIE'S EGGPLANT CASSEROLE +   Preparation: 30 minutes
                                      Cooking: 30 minutes

Too many ingredients? You hate eggplant? (See COMMENT.) But this is a major Venetian masterpiece!! It has a mildly spicy, what-is-it flavor, and it's delicious hot, warm, cold. Cook it for a long weekend. Cajole a friend into helping. This recipe makes a big batch. There will be plenty left over for other nights or lunches. Or use reheated leftovers as a vegetable side dish. Nibble it cold for breakfast. It freezes well, too.

LINE UP YOUR INGREDIENTS:

1-lb. eggplant   15-oz. jar marinara sauce
½ cup rice   4 oz. Cheddar cheese, shredded
2 large onions   4 tablespoons grated Parmesan or
2 green peppers   Romano cheese
½ lb. mushrooms (optional)   1 teaspoon salt
2 cloves garlic   ¼ teaspoon pepper
4 tablespoons cooking oil

PREPARATION:

In this recipe the whole eggplant bakes 30 minutes in oven, and the rice cooks on stove top while you prepare the vegetables. Then everything's ready to assemble in a large skillet to be cooked together on stove top for a half hour.

Turn oven to 350.

Put whole, unpeeled eggplant on pie plate. Place on center rack of oven. Bake 30 minutes. Remove to counter. (Looks awful.)

Let it cool 5 minutes. Slice off ends. Don't peel; in pie pan, slice and chop it up in big chunks. Put aside.

While eggplant bakes, cook rice in saucepan in 1¼ cups of water: Bring to a boil. Add and stir rice. When boiling, turn down heat to low. Cover. Cook 18 minutes. Put aside.

While eggplant bakes and rice simmers, peel and chop up onion. Remove seeds and stem of green peppers; slice/chop peppers.

Slice mushrooms. Peel and chop garlic.

In large iron 12" skillet, heat oil over medium heat. When hot add onions, garlic, green pepper, and mushrooms. Fry, stirring now and then, for 5 minutes. Don't brown anything.

Add eggplant, rice, marinara sauce, Cheddar cheese, and salt and pepper. Stir thoroughly. Top with grated Parmesan.

Cover with lid, or with aluminum foil wrapped air-tight. Cook over low heat for 30 minutes.

+ COMMENT +

Eggplant is substantial, and cheap. It's worth learning to love. Always hideously gray when cooked, but most good eggplant recipes include cheerful red tomatoes.

+ + + + + + + + + + +

+ LENTILS +   Takes 30 minutes

Start these early, as they take a while. If you've never tasted lentils except in soup, you're in for a nice surprise. They're firm and slightly peppery. They're also protein-rich. (Check package directions; buy lentils that do not need to be soaked.)

Combine ½ cup lentils with 1½ cups water plus ¼ teaspoon salt. Bring to boil over high heat. Turn to low. Cover. Simmer 30 minutes, or till lentils are tender. Drain into sieve at sink. Add 2 tablespoons butter and 2 chopped-up scallions. Stir. Cover. Let wait a few (5) minutes. Serve.

+ + + + + + + + + + +

+ HOT FRENCH BREAD +

For 2 people, buy 1 or 2 hero-size French breads. Slice into 1½" chunks, encase in foil, heat in a 350 oven for 15 minutes. Butter chunks immediately. Leftovers reheated are even better than the first time around. Reheat gently.

+ +
MENU (serves 2):   Dilled Fish in Foil
                   Home-Fried Potatoes (page 74)
                   Tossed Green Salad with Diced Tomatoes
                       (page 30)
                   Traditional French Dressing (page 31)
+ +

+ DILLED FISH IN FOIL +   Preparation: 10 minutes
                                             Baking: 30 minutes

If you were served this in a fine restaurant, you would not believe how childishly simple
it is to prepare. It brews its own private gourmet sauce. Make a well-sealed envelope and
you'll have NO pan to wash (much).

   LINE UP YOUR INGREDIENTS:

1 lb. thin fish fillets (fluke, flounder, sole,   3-oz. package cream cheese, softened
      whiting, or turbot; unlike the fine   (room temperature)
      restaurant, choose according to   1 teaspoon dillweed (not -seed)
      price)   Salt and pepper
4-6 paper-thin slices of lemon, unpeeled

   PREPARATION:

   Turn oven to 400.
   Cut off enough aluminum foil to enfold the fish completely. Place foil in a small
roasting pan and put the fish flat on it.
   Crumble cream cheese all over top of fish and alongside.
   Place lemon slices down the center. Sprinkle with dill. Salt and pepper lightly.
   Fold over the foil and pinch it together air-tight.
   Bake on center rack of oven at 400 for 30 minutes. Remove. Spoon creamy sauce over
fish.
   Serve right from foil onto plates.

+ COMMENT +

You could add very finely minced onion to fish before the cream cheese.

                         + + + + + + + + + + + +

+ HOME-FRIED POTATOES +   Takes 1 hour, or less

This two-step method ensures a good result, but you'll need to be attentive at the end.

INGREDIENTS:

3 medium-size potatoes, unpeeled   1 tablespoon cooking oil
1 medium onion   Salt and pepper
1 tablespoon butter

PREPARATION:

Put potatoes in saucepan. Cover well with water. Bring to a hard boil. Time for 15
minutes' boiling, or till a kitchen fork pierces the center easily. Drain. Leave potatoes on
counter for 5 minutes to cool.

Peel and chop up onion.

Melt butter and oil together in 8" skillet over medium-high heat. Meanwhile, peel
potatoes. Chunk them into skillet in large pieces, bite-size.

Sprinkle chopped onion over top of potatoes. Cover pan and continue to cook for 5
minutes. Uncover, add salt and pepper sparingly and, using a wide spatula, scoop
potatoes up from bottom and flip over. This gives the top side a chance to brown.

Cook 15 minutes more, uncovered, stirring now and then till nicely browned. Serve.

+ +
SATURDAY - Fourth Week - SATURDAY - Fourth Week - SATURDAY - Fourth Week -
+ +

+ +
MENU (serves 2):   Baked Cottage Ham Butt
                          Southern-Style Cabbage
                          Easy Corn Fritters
+ +

+ BAKED COTTAGE HAM BUTT +   Baking: 1½ to 2 hours (check directions on
                                    wrapping)

There's nothing to this. It's a tender, succulent cut of meat that bakes and bastes itself
while you go elsewhere for an hour or 2.

LINE UP YOUR INGREDIENTS:

2-lb. cottage ham butt; one that feels firm will be leanest

PREPARATION:

Remove ham's wrapping and inner casing.
Put ham on rack in 9" × 13" roasting pan.
Place on center rack of oven.
Bake at 350 for 1½ hours (or follow directions printed on outer wrapping). Remove
from oven, put on serving dish. Save juices in pan to make Southern-style Cabbage.

+ COMMENT +

Leftover ham makes wonderful **MACARONI AND HAM CASSEROLE**: Cook 1½ cups elbow
macaroni. Drain it. Put it in a greased casserole. Cut ham into bite-size pieces (1-2 cups).
Add to macaroni; stir. Turn oven to 350. Use recipe on page 137 for Mornay Sauce. Make
it and add to the macaroni. Sprinkle on 2-3 tablespoons grated Parmesan cheese. Bake,
covered, 30 minutes.

+ + + + + + + + + + +

+ SOUTHERN-STYLE CABBAGE +   Takes 25 minutes

Right in the same pan where the ham cooked, you stir the cut-up cabbage till it
"marries" with all those delectable ham juices. Ruthie says, "It's so easy, it's kid stuff."
   Cut up ½ head of a small (1-lb.) cabbage into bite-size (small) pieces. Discard core.
Put pieces into the roasting pan where the ham cooked. On medium heat, stir a bit for 5
minutes. Turn heat to low. Cook 15 minutes more. Stir now and then. Remove from heat.
Taste. Add salt and pepper if necessary.

+ COMMENT +

Keep ham warm on platter in OFF oven till cabbage is cooked and fritters are flipped
(see next recipe).

+ + + + + + + + + + +

+ EASY CORN FRITTERS +   Takes 10 minutes

Fritters plain are perfect with ham. Good for breakfast, not so plain, with jam.

   INGREDIENTS:

1 egg   8-oz. can creamed corn
½ cup self-rising flour   2 tablespoons oil (corn)

   PREPARATION:

   In mixing bowl: Beat egg till creamy. Add flour and corn. Stir to mix thoroughly.
   In 8" skillet, measure 1 tablespoon oil over medium heat. Warm a minute.
   Use a tablespoon: Put 4-5 tablespoons of fritter batter in skillet. (Each tablespoonful
separate.) Fry till golden brown on bottoms. Turn with a spatula. Fry other sides.
Remove to a plate.
   Fry second batch of fritters the same way, using a small amount of additional oil if
skillet seems dry. Serve.
   This recipe makes 18-20 little fritters.

JUST DESSERTS

HERE ARE SOME LYRICAL fantasies and a clinker or two (which you may prefer). They are all easily prepared, require <u>no</u> elaborate construction, exotic ingredients, or weird equipment. They will ruin your teeth and are perfectly delicious.

+ + + + + + + + + + +

+ <u>McCRYSTLE'S MIDNIGHT SHOTGUN SPECIAL</u> +

Preparation: 5-10 minutes
Baking: 350 for 30 minutes

It's 11:15 P.M. and you're dying for something quick and deliciously sweet. Here's a fudgy coconut brownie you can eat right out of the oven and it will hold up well at room temperature for days. Keep it in the pan, covered <u>air-tight</u>.

LINE UP YOUR INGREDIENTS:

2 eggs
½ cup (1 stick) margarine or butter
1 cup sugar
1 cup flour
4 tablespoons cocoa

¼ cup cream of coconut (comes in a can)
1 can (3½-oz.) grated coconut, approximately

PREPARATION:

Turn oven to 350.
In large mixing bowl, beat eggs.
In small saucepan, melt butter.
Add all ingredients to eggs: sugar, flour, melted butter, cocoa, cream of coconut, and coconut. Mix very thoroughly together with wooden spoon.
Grease a 9″ × 9″ square cake pan. Pour in cake batter.
Bake at 350, on center rack of oven, for 30 minutes.

+ + + + + + + + + + + +

+ <u>APPLE CRISP</u> +

Preparation: 15 minutes
Baking: 45 minutes

<u>Serves 6</u>. For apple towns and apple lovers, in the fall and winter: It's hot, and cinnamony, and mushy, and crisp, with ice cream oozing over it. Very satisfying.

No weird equipment is required.
++++++++++++++++++

INGREDIENTS:

6 tart, large apples (Courtland,
    McIntosh, Granny Smith)
½ cup sugar
¼ teaspoon ground cloves (optional)
½ teaspoon cinnamon
2 teaspoons lemon juice
2 teaspoons vanilla extract

½ cup brown sugar
¾ cup sifted flour
⅛ teaspoon salt
6 tablespoons butter or margarine
¼ cup (2 oz.) chopped walnuts (or
    pecans)
1 pint vanilla ice cream

PREPARATION:

Turn oven to 350.

Grease a 2-quart casserole with butter or margarine.

Quarter apples. Remove cores. Don't bother to peel. Cut quarters in thirds. Put in casserole.

Sprinkle over apples the sugar, cloves, cinnamon, lemon juice, and vanilla. Turn and mix, with hands, till apples are well coated.

In a large mixing bowl, measure and blend the brown sugar, flour (sift through a strainer into bowl), salt, and butter in small slices. Mix lightly with fingertips till butter is crumbly.

Put mixture on top of apples. Pat down to even.

Sprinkle chopped nuts on top.

Bake at 350 on center rack of oven, uncovered, for 45 minutes or till crust (nuts) are browned. Or, after baking, put under broiler briefly to brown (1 minute maximum).

Serve warm with scoops of vanilla ice cream on top. Sheer bliss.

+ + + + + + + + + + + +

+ OLD-FASHIONED ICEBOX CAKE +   Takes 5 minutes

You make this the night before, refrigerate, and let the whipped cream work its magic. Next day you have a fudgy, chocolate confection worthy of its longtime fame.

LINE UP YOUR INGREDIENTS:

1 pint whipping cream
2 teaspoons sugar

1 teaspoon vanilla
1 box (8½-oz.) Nabisco chocolate wafers
    (cookies)

PREPARATION:

In mixing bowl, with rotary beater, beat cream, sugar, and vanilla together till cream stands in points when you withdraw beater.

Arrange wafers in a 9″ pie pan to make first layer. Top with a layer of cream.

Continue to layer wafers and cream until all wafers are used up. End with a topping of cream.

Save one last wafer to crumble over the top of cream for elegant effect. Refrigerate at least 8 hours. Overnight is best.

+ + + + + + + + + + +

+ <u>ANONYMOUS (A CAKE)</u> +   Preparation: 15 minutes
                                        Baking: 35 minutes

<u>Serves 6-8</u>. We have named this cake after the world-famous poet because it is passionate, sensuous, secret, and a bit mushy. It's also irresistible. No one will guess the ingredients, so don't alarm people with the details.

INGREDIENTS:

8-oz. can crushed pineapple
8-oz. can apricots
3-oz. package shredded coconut,
    approximately

1-lb., 2-oz. box yellow cake mix
3-oz. package chopped walnuts or pecans
2 sticks (½ lb.) margarine

PREPARATION:

Grease a 9″ × 9″ cake pan.
Turn oven to 350.
Layer the ingredients into cake pan as follows:
<u>1st layer</u>: Both cans of fruit <u>plus</u> juices. Spread fruit evenly on bottom of pan.
<u>2nd layer</u>: Sprinkle coconut over all, evenly.
<u>3rd layer</u>: Sprinkle dry cake mix evenly over coconut.
<u>4th layer</u>: Scatter <u>chopped-up</u> walnuts on top of cake mix.
<u>5th layer</u>: Cut up margarine in 1-tablespoon slices and lay evenly all over top of nuts.
Bake on center rack of 350 oven for 35 minutes.
Remove to counter. Let cool 10 minutes. Serve right from pan.

+ <u>COMMENT</u> +

The dry cake mix absorbs the juices on pan bottom and turns into a cake.

+ + + + + + + + + + +

+ <u>GRAPES IN BROWN-SUGAR CREAM</u> +   Takes 10 minutes

<u>Serves 6</u>. This simple combination has enormous grace and style. Each ingredient brings out flavor of the other two. Practically Post Graduate sophisticated. Everyone likes it, so will you. (A super summertime treat.)

INGREDIENTS:

1½ lbs. <u>SEEDLESS</u> grapes (light green)   1 cup (½ pint) sour cream
½ cup brown sugar

PREPARATION:

Rinse grapes quickly under cold tap water. Drain. Dry on paper towels. Remove all stems.
In large bowl, mix brown sugar and sour cream. Blend well.
Add grapes to bowl. Stir gently to coat all grapes.
Refrigerate 1 hour, or more. Serve icy cold.

+ + + + + + + + + + +

+ <u>PEACH SHORTCAKE EXPRESS</u> +   Preparation: 5 minutes
   Baking: 15-20 minutes

<u>Serves 6</u>. Here's a weird way to arrive at a shortcake. <u>Start</u> with the ice cream. Soon
you'll have a high and light, sweet muffin. Nice halved and toasted, plain. Serve with
your favorite, or nearest favorite, fruit. (If you love strawberries, look at the price.)

INGREDIENTS:

1 cup MUSHY vanilla ice cream   3 ripe peaches (or a 1-lb. can of sliced
Butter   peaches)
1 cup self-rising flour   ½ pint heavy cream
2 tablespoons sugar

PREPARATION:

Let ice cream get mushy at room temperature.
Turn oven to 400.
With butter, lightly grease six muffin cups (housewares stores have these).
Mix melted ice cream, flour, and sugar together well in a bowl. Put in muffin cups.
Bake at 400 on center rack of oven for 15-20 minutes, or till tops are light brown.
Remove.
Let cool 5 minutes. Cut in half, through the middle.
Peel peaches. Slice. (Use ½ a peach per person.) Put slices on bottom piece of
shortcake. Top with upper half.
Pour cream over top, or whip cream and spoon on.

+ <u>COMMENT</u> +

You can use defrosted frozen peaches or other fruit. Defrosting will take 1-2 hours on
counter top.

+ + + + + + + + + + +

+ HASTY MOCHA ICING +   Takes 10 minutes

This lick-the-bowl icing melts in your mouth. It turns an ordinary store-bought cake into a "supreme confection."

LINE UP YOUR INGREDIENTS:

1 pound cake, angel cake or sponge cake
1 package instant chocolate pudding

1 tablespoon dry instant coffee
1½ pints (3 cups) light cream

PREPARATION:

Put cake on large plate. Cut it (horizontally) into 2 or 3 layers.

In mixing bowl, stir pudding, coffee, and cream until the icing thickens (use an eggbeater, or electric beater at low speed) for 2 minutes. Let it thicken in bowl a few minutes more.

Spoon mixture evenly between layers, all over top, and along sides.

Refrigerate about an hour or overnight.

+ + + + + + + + + + +

+ FLORIAN APPLEGATE'S   Preparation: 5 minutes
HOT FUDGE SAUCE +   Cooking: 10 minutes

If you have a yearning for old-fashioned, gooey, hot fudge sauce slathered over vanilla ice cream, this is it. What you don't use today keeps in a jar in the refrigerator for weeks.

LINE UP YOUR INGREDIENTS:

1 tablespoon butter
2 oz. unsweetened chocolate, or 2
      packets Nestlé's Choco-Bake
⅓ cup hot water

1 cup granulated sugar
2 tablespoons light corn syrup
1 teaspoon vanilla

PREPARATION:

In a small saucepan, over LOW heat, melt butter and chocolate. When soft and oozy, slowly add hot water, sugar, and corn syrup. Stir as you add.

On high heat, bring to a boil. Stir.

Boil steadily, but not furiously, for 5-8 minutes for a thicker sauce. DO NOT STIR. Remove from heat. Add vanilla. Stir well.

+ <u>COMMENT</u> +

To keep warm: Put pan in larger pan of hot water.

+ + + + + + + + + + +

+ <u>BLUEBERRY COBBLER</u> +   Preparation: 15 minutes
                                               Baking: 25 minutes

<u>Serves 6</u>. This is a tart-sweet pudding with a crisp, golden biscuit hat. Make and bake in
an ovenproof mixing bowl.

INGREDIENTS:

2 boxes frozen berries (blueberries,   1 tablespoon sugar
    strawberries, or raspberries)   1½ teaspoons baking powder
1 tablespoon cornstarch   ¼ teaspoon salt
1½ teaspoons lemon juice   3 tablespoons butter
½ teaspoon ground cinnamon   ⅓ cup milk
1 cup flour   1 egg

PREPARATION:

In a 2-quart saucepan, put fruit, cornstarch, lemon juice, and cinnamon. Cook over
medium heat till berries defrost and mixture is bubbly. Cook and stir together for 5
minutes. Pour into a 1½- or 2-quart Pyrex bowl or casserole.

Turn oven to 400.

In a large mixing bowl, measure in the flour, sugar, baking powder, and salt. Stir dry
ingredients to mix together well.

Cut butter into dry ingredients. Rub through with your fingers to blend well, till
mixture is crumbly.

In a cup, beat egg with a fork, lightly.

Add milk to egg. Stir to mix.

Add the wet mixture to the dry mixture in mixing bowl, and stir till all is gooey. Drop
this on top of berries with a large spoon.

Bake on center rack of oven at 400 for 25 minutes. (Don't cover.)

Cool, and serve. Good topped with ice cream, heavy cream, sour cream, or <u>plain</u>
yogurt.

+ <u>COMMENT</u> +

If you've bought FRESH berries (1 quart): Add ¼ cup of sugar at the start, before you
begin cooking them.

ALWAYS ON SUNDAY

+ BRUNCH: DATING, 1980s STYLE +

WINE AND ROSES plus lobsters for 2 cost too much money to invest in a brand-new date, and they are entirely unnecessary with an old friend.

Movies? Who wants to pay for a movie when it's just another way of sitting alone?

Invite him/her for Sunday brunch. In the casual* setting of your own place, you'll pick up a lot of useful character information. The more comfortable and informal you are, the more relaxed the date will be.

One person can stylishly handle the following recipes for 2 or more, but guests are usually eager to assist. Let them.

+ THE MENU +

Prepare in advance whatever portions of selected recipes you can. A table already set makes you look in control and at ease. Try fruit or fruit juice for starters. Maybe, to stun your guest, produce Stephanie's Perfect Banana Bread, or a light dessert (Grapes in Brown-Sugar Cream). If you want to resort to the store-bought, a nice coffee cake warmed in the oven and served with sweet butter is always welcome.

+ + + + + + + + + + +

+ COWBOY EGGS +

Preparation: 10 minutes
Cooking: 25 minutes

You find these on menus in the Southwestern U.S., where they are firecracker hot, under the name "Huevos Rancheros." Here's a milder version that you can stimulate by adding more chili powder or chopped, canned jalapeño peppers. You can make the sauce the day before, refrigerate. Reheat, add eggs and cheese.

LINE UP YOUR INGREDIENTS:

¼ cup olive oil, or any cooking oil
2 medium garlic cloves, peeled, halved
2 medium onions, chopped
2 medium green peppers, seeded,
    chopped
1-lb. can tomatoes, pulp only
½ teaspoon salt

½ teaspoon black pepper
2 teaspoons chili powder
½ teaspoon oregano
4-6 eggs
4-6 slices cheese, Monterey Jack,
    mozzarella, Cheddar (optional)

---

*We visualize creative clutter. Also, if you aren't anywhere near New York, the Sunday New York Times lying around is exceptionally effective.

PREPARATION:

Heat 12" skillet. Add oil and garlic cloves. Remove garlic with slotted spoon after 1 minute.

Add chopped onions and peppers. Cook and stir over medium heat for 5 minutes. Add tomato pulp, salt, pepper, chili powder, oregano.

Cook this mixture, uncovered, breaking up tomato pieces, until it is thick and not watery. About 15-20 minutes.

When ready to add eggs, make 4 or more indentations with the back of a spoon in the sauce. Open eggs into these. Now cover pan with a lid. Cook eggs until tops are set the way you like them.

Off heat, cover top with cheese if you want to use it. Re-cover with lid until cheese has melted.

+ COMMENTS +

1. Drink tomato juice from can.
2. You can slide skillet under broiler to melt cheese.

+ + + + + + + + + + + +

+ HUGO'S CHICKEN LIVERS SUPREME +   Preparation: 5 minutes
                                     Cooking: 10 minutes

Serves 2-4. One could become rhapsodic over the tantalizing breakfast scents which waft around as these cook. Marvelously tasty, and quick. Serve with scrambled eggs.

LINE UP YOUR INGREDIENTS:

4 slices bacon   ½ lb. chicken livers (about 8)
1 large onion, chopped   Salt and pepper
½ teaspoon thyme

PREPARATION:

Cut bacon in 1" pieces.

In 8" skillet, fry bacon over medium-high heat 2-3 minutes. (Stir around now and then.)

Add onion and thyme. Fry 3-4 minutes until onions are golden. Stir a bit.

Add livers. Fry, and stir a bit again, for 3-4 minutes more, or till all pink disappears and livers are brown but not stiff. Salt and pepper. Serve immediately, or cover and keep warm on counter till eggs are scrambled.

+ + + + + + + + + + + +

The more comfortable and informal you are,
the more relaxed your date will be.

+ +

+ <u>PEASANT OMELET</u> +   Takes 15 minutes

<u>Serves 4.</u> The peasant is French, in case you wondered.

3 strips bacon
1 regular can whole cooked potatoes,
    well drained

2-3 tablespoons frozen chives, or 2
    chopped fresh scallions
6 eggs, beaten in bowl
Salt and pepper

PREPARATION:

In large skillet, fry bacon until crisp; drain on paper.
Slice potatoes thin, add to hot pan grease, fry until golden and somewhat crisp.
Mix chives in bowl with eggs. Pour on top of potatoes in pan. Add salt and pepper.
Lift edges of omelet to let top liquid run under.
When all is <u>somewhat</u> cooked, add crumbled bacon.
Slide skillet under broiler for a FEW seconds to cook top. <u>Don't overcook.</u>

+ <u>COMMENT</u> +

Leftover boiled potatoes are better than canned.

+ + + + + + + + + + + +

+ <u>CHIPPED BEEF ON TOAST</u> +

<u>Serves 2 or 3.</u> Buy a 3-4 oz. package <u>chipped beef</u>, or the butcher will slice some for you.
Make sure you're buying "chipped beef" and not one of the many imitations.

PREPARATION:

Tear beef to shreds, with fingers.

Heat a small skillet over medium heat. Add 2 tablespoons butter or margarine. When melted, add shredded beef.

Toss it in pan to coat. Sprinkle in 2 tablespoons flour, stir again until beef is thoroughly incorporated with butter and flour. Slowly pour in 1 cup milk, and 1 tablespoon Worcestershire sauce. Now stir constantly until all is thick and creamy. Do NOT add salt. Serve on dry toast.

+ + + + + + + + + + +

+ CRUSTLESS SQUARE QUICHE +   Preparation: 15 minutes
                                     Cooking: 35 minutes

Serves 2-4. This slices into portions like a regular quiche, without the bother of making a crust. Serve it with fresh fruit and buttered toast. Use an 8″ × 8″ square cake pan.

LINE UP YOUR INGREDIENTS:

2 tablespoons prepared bread crumbs
2 slices bacon
4 eggs
1 small onion

½ cup (4 oz.) shredded Swiss or Cheddar cheese
1 cup (½ pint) half-and-half cream

PREPARATION:

Turn oven to 350.

Grease bottom and sides of pan thoroughly. Add bread crumbs. Shake around till they stick to the bottom and sides of pan.

Fry the bacon in small skillet. Crumble bacon. Set aside.

Beat eggs in large mixing bowl. Add crumbled bacon.

Peel and chop onion. Add to eggs. Add shredded cheese and cream. Mix well.

Pour all into greased pan. Bake on center rack of 350 oven for 30-35 minutes, or until a knife inserted gently comes out clean. Remove from oven.

Leave on counter top 5 minutes before cutting into squares.

+ COMMENTS +

1. This can also be made in a well-buttered and crumbed 8″ round pie pan (9″ is too large).

2. You can substitute 3 scallions for the onion; chop up the whites and most of the green parts.

3. Light or medium cream will make this even richer - and more expensive.

+ + + + + + + + + + +

EL CHEEPO PARTIES

A PARTY IS SIMPLY a sharing. It doesn't call for titanic effort and nail-biting: The getting together is the important part. You can easily afford each of the menus here (if you don't feed 45 people). Most of the recipes originated in poorer parts of the world where invention was a necessity. Try the ones you've never heard of, O ye of little faith. Everyone will ask for the recipes. Tell them to buy the book.

To add to all party menus, see recipes for heated-up breads in INDEX.

Cheese and fruit may sound like a good dessert idea for a party, but they usually aren't. Expensive, and people are too busy talking to peel, cut, and concentrate on cheese and fruit (a POST GRADUATE taste). Serve them something all-too-easy to eat up from the chapter JUST DESSERTS.

And there are more feed-a-crowd recipes in BY POPULAR DEMAND.

+ +
PARTY #1 - PARTY #1 - PARTY #1 - PARTY #1 - PARTY #1 - PARTY #1 - PARTY #1 -
+ +

+ + + + + + + + + + + + + + + + + + + +
MENU (serves 6-8):   Guacamole
                           Jenny's Enchiladas
                           Jenny's Mexican Rice
+ + + + + + + + + + + + + + + + + + + +

TIMING INFORMATION:

The Guacamole must be made in advance to get icy cold.
Enchiladas may be prepared ahead up to the point of the 30 minutes' baking.
Rice: Get the rice started shortly before you put the enchiladas in to bake.

+ GUACAMOLE +   Takes 10 minutes
                                    Refrigerate: 1 hour at least

A Dip. Most guacamole is smooth. This version has a nice range of textures: the silky avocado, sharp onion bits, and icy little tomato chunks. A famous recipe.

INGREDIENTS:

2 large ripe avocados (soft but not mushy)	2 ripe tomatoes
	½ teaspoon vinegar
1 medium onion	½ teaspoon salt

PREPARATION:

Cut avocados in half, pry out pits. (Save 1 pit.) Scoop out avocado meat, mash in a bowl with a fork.

Peel and chop up onion, fine. Add to bowl.

Peel tomatoes. (To do this easily, put tomatoes in a pan of boiling hot water for 1 minute. After that uncomfortable immersion, the skin slips right off - as whose wouldn't!)

Cut tomatoes in small pieces and add to mashed avocado.

Measure in vinegar and salt. Stir well. Bury reserved pit in center of mixture, which keeps it green, mysteriously.

Refrigerate for an hour or longer. Before serving, discard pit. (Unsightly.)

Use as your party dip, with Fritos.

+ COMMENTS +

1. This is weird! If your avocados are hard and you need to ripen them right now, pronto - here's how: Bring some water to a boil. Turn it down to low. Simmer the avocados 4-5 minutes. Olé! You can fool Mother Nature!

2. The windowsill caper: Hard avocados ripen on a sunny windowsill in 2-3 days.

3. If you want enough of this for a salad for 8, increase ingredients to 3 ripe avocados, 3 medium-size ripe tomatoes, and add more salt to taste. Place dollops of guacamole on lettuce leaves.

+ + + + + + + + + + + +

+ JENNY'S ENCHILADAS +   Preparation: 30 minutes
                                     Cooking: 30 minutes

Serves 6-8. Jennifer says, "It's a half hour making, and a half hour baking." One way to cut down "making" time: Find a willing slave.

LINE UP YOUR INGREDIENTS:

1 cup peanut or corn oil   1 package corn tortillas (12 in package)

SAUCE:

¼ cup oil   8-oz. can tomato sauce
1 medium onion   8-oz. can Mexican chili sauce
4 cloves garlic   ½ teaspoon EACH chili powder, cumin,
4 scallions   and salt

FILLING:

1 pint small-curd cottage cheese
½ pint sour cream
4 scallions
1 can (1 lb., 2 oz.) WHOLE KERNEL corn
     niblets

Small can black pitted olives (optional)
Salt and pepper
2 tablespoons wheat germ (optional)
8 oz. shredded Cheddar cheese

PREPARATION:

To do Sauce: In 2-quart saucepan, warm oil over medium heat. Peel and chop onion. Add it. Peel and chop garlic. Add it. Stir together and cook till onions are limp, 2-3 minutes.

Remove root ends of 4 scallions; chop up white and ¾ of green part. Add to pan; cook 2 minutes more.

Add tomato sauce, chili sauce, chili powder, cumin, and salt.

Turn heat to low. Cover. Simmer 10 minutes. Turn off heat. Uncover to let cool a bit.

To do Filling: In large mixing bowl, put cottage cheese, sour cream, 4 MORE scallions all chopped up (green and white part), DRAINED can of corn, drained can of olives (halved), salt, pepper, and wheat germ.

Mix all together well.

ASSEMBLING:

Turn oven to 325.

In 8″ skillet, put cup of peanut oil. Bring it to bubbly (about 1 minute over high heat). Turn heat to medium.

One at a time, "deep fry" tortillas in hot oil (30 seconds on each side). Dip in warm red sauce to coat both sides, stack on plate to keep warm.

When all are sauced, transfer tortillas one at a time to baking dish (see COMMENT). Spoon 3 tablespoons of cottage-cheese mixture down center, and roll tortilla (like a bed roll). Slide it, seam side down, to end of baking dish, making room for additional side-by-side rolls.

Continue in this hectic fashion until all 12 tortillas are filled and rolled. (Here's where an extra pair of hands really helps!)

Now, pour the SAUCE over everything; it must cover completely. Top with shredded Cheddar cheese; sprinkle it over all evenly.

You can do all ahead up to this point. Refrigerate. To finish at dinnertime, bake, uncovered, at 350 for 30 minutes.

+ COMMENT +

Your 13″ × 9″ × 2″ roasting pan will do for this recipe, but it's a bit small and things will be snug. A little longer dish or pan would be better.

+ + + + + + + + + + + +

+ <u>JENNY'S MEXICAN RICE</u> +   Preparation: 15 minutes
                                   Cooking: 35 minutes

<u>Serves 6-8</u>. This colorful rice dish helps set a pretty table. It is authentically Mexican, and you can give it as much of that South-of-the-Border zip as you like with the Tabasco.

LINE UP YOUR INGREDIENTS:

10-oz. package frozen peas
1 medium onion
2 cloves garlic
3 tablespoons peanut or corn oil
2 cups white rice (Uncle Ben's
     converted)

4 cups chicken broth (use 4 tablespoons
     instant chicken bouillon mix and 4
     cups hot water)
3 tomatoes
½ teaspoon salt
Tabasco sauce (optional and to taste)

PREPARATION:

Open frozen peas. Let sit on counter to defrost.
Peel and chop up onion and garlic. Slice and chop tomatoes.
In 2-quart saucepan, heat oil on medium-high heat (1 minute). Add onion and garlic. Stir and fry 3 minutes.
Add rice. Stir 1-2 minutes, or till rice is covered with butter and opaque (no longer chalky white).
Add chicken broth. Bring to boil on high heat. Cover. Turn to low. Simmer 20 minutes.
Add peas, tomatoes, salt, and 2-3 dashes of Tabasco sauce. (Mild. If you want fire, add Tabasco and taste to desired incandescence.) Stir well into rice. Cover.
Cook 3-4 minutes till veggies are heated through.
Serve, as is. Or top with any leftover enchilada sauce.

+ <u>COMMENT</u> +

You can make rice ahead. Reserve thawed peas. Add peas and reheat on <u>low</u> heat for 10 minutes, stirring now and then.

+ +
PARTY #2 - PARTY #2 - PARTY #2 - PARTY #2 - PARTY #2 - PARTY #2 - PARTY #2 -
+ +

+ +
MENU (serves 6-8):   Serbian Presnack
                          "George" (a Salad)
+ +

TIMING INFORMATION:

"<u>George</u>" must be made 6 hours or more in advance for flavors to mingle. <u>Presnack</u> may be prepared early; bake it just before serving.

A party doesn't call for titanic effort.

++++++++++++++++++++

A party is simply a sharing.

++++++++++++++++

+ <u>SERBIAN PRESNACK</u> + Takes 50 minutes in all

<u>Serves 6-8</u>. Olivia says this looks like a flat quiche. It does. You cut it in squares and eat it with your fingers.

LINE UP YOUR INGREDIENTS:

1½ sticks butter	1 teaspoon baking powder
¾ lb. Monterey Jack cheese	½ cup flour
2 small (3 oz.) packages cream cheese	½ lb. cottage cheese with chives
6 eggs	½ teaspoon EACH salt, pepper, paprika

PREPARATION:

Grease a 13″ × 9″ × 2″ flat roasting pan. Turn oven to 375.

Cube (dice) the first three ingredients: butter, Monterey Jack, and cream cheese. Strew them evenly on bottom of roasting pan.

In large mixing bowl, beat eggs with a whisk or beater.

To eggs add baking powder, flour, cottage cheese, and salt, pepper, and paprika. Mix well with spoon. Spread over ingredients in pan and pat even.

Bake at 375 for 40 minutes.

+ + + + + + + + + + + +

+ "GEORGE" (A SALAD) +

Serves 6-8. When long-haired John Lennon first came to the U.S., a reporter sneered, "And what do you call that kind of a haircut?" Lennon replied, "I just call it George." You can't argue with a remark like that. So, this independent-minded, multi-layered salad is called "George." To serve it, you scoop to the bottom with a large spoon to get up all the layers. You can make it from 6 to even 36 hours in advance. Cover with plastic wrap and refrigerate.

INGREDIENTS (in the order in which they are layered):

¼ small head iceberg lettuce, shredded
¼ teaspoon EACH salt, pepper, sugar
½ green pepper, chopped
½ bag (5 oz.) fresh spinach, stems
   removed, shredded
¼ teaspoon EACH salt, pepper, sugar
   (this is a repeat)

3 hard-boiled eggs, chopped
6 red radishes, sliced thin
10-oz. package frozen peas, thawed (raw)
1 red onion, peeled and sliced thin
12 medium-size mushrooms, sliced thin
¼ small head iceberg lettuce, shredded
   (this is a repeat)

Layer ingredients in a <u>large</u> mixing bowl, in order given above. Top evenly with the dressing. Refrigerate covered.

+ DRESSING +

½ pint <u>Hellmann's mayonnaise</u> mixed well with ½ cup (4 oz.) <u>sour cream</u>. May be spiked with <u>lemon juice</u>, <u>pepper</u>, <u>herbs</u>.

+ +
+ +

+ + + + + + + + + + + + + + + + + + + +
MENU (serves 6):   Pastitsio
                       Spinach Salad A+
+ + + + + + + + + + + + + + + + + + + +

TIMING INFORMATION:

Make <u>Pastitsio</u> in advance; bake just before serving. <u>Spinach Salad A+</u> may be assembled in the bowl; toss with dressing at the table.

+ PASTITSIO +
                                   Preparation: 20 minutes
                                   Cooking: 40 minutes

Serves 6. Greek in origin. Layers of macaroni and beef are covered with a cheesy cream sauce. This is rich, goes a long way. Pronounce "Pastitsio" any way you want to.

LINE UP YOUR INGREDIENTS:

½ lb. (8 oz.) elbow macaroni
2 medium chopped onions
4 tablespoons butter
1 lb. chopped beef
1 large tomato
1 teaspoon oregano
½ teaspoon cinnamon

⅛ teaspoon nutmeg (optional)
1 teaspoon salt
¼ teaspoon pepper
¾ cup grated Romano or Parmesan cheese
2 tablespoons flour
1 cup milk
1 egg

PREPARATION:

In large pot, boil macaroni according to package directions. Drain over sink into large sieve or colander.

Meanwhile, peel and chop onions. Melt HALF the butter (2 tablespoons) in 8″ skillet over medium-high heat. Add onions to skillet. Stir 2-3 minutes.

Add beef to skillet. Stir and fry till all pink disappears from beef.

Chop tomato. Add to beef with the oregano, cinnamon, nutmeg, salt, and pepper. Cover, cook on low heat, 10 minutes.

Uncover, mix in ½ cup grated cheese. Blend well together. Remove from heat.

Butter a deep 3-quart casserole liberally on bottom and sides. Layer in macaroni, then meat mixture; then macaroni, then meat, etc.

SAUCE:

In small saucepan, melt remaining 2 tablespoons butter over medium-low heat. Measure in flour and stir well. Remove from heat.

Slowly add milk, stirring all the time with a whisk.

Add the rest of the grated cheese. Cook over medium-low heat till thickened (3-4 minutes). Stir constantly.

In small bowl, beat egg. Add to sauce. Stir well to blend egg into sauce.

Pour sauce into casserole. Cover casserole. Bake at 350 for 30 minutes.

+ + + + + + + + + + + +

+ SPINACH SALAD A+ +   Takes 15 minutes

Serves 6. One of the prettiest and tastiest of green salads. The rich, dark, shining green leaves look so fresh - and stay perkier than regular lettuce.

INGREDIENTS:

10-oz. package fresh spinach
3 eggs
6 slices bacon
Small can water chestnuts
14-oz. can bean sprouts

¼ cup red-wine vinegar
1 cup salad oil (olive or corn)
1 clove garlic, crushed
½ teaspoon salt
½ teaspoon Dijon mustard
¼ teaspoon pepper

PREPARATION:

Rinse spinach. Remove stems and discard. Dry spinach thoroughly between 2 towels. Tear leaves into bite-size pieces and put in large salad bowl.

Put eggs in saucepan with cold water to cover. Bring to a boil over high heat. Turn down to medium-low heat. Boil 15 minutes. Cool under cold tap, and peel. Set aside.

Meanwhile, fry bacon till crisp. Drain on paper towel. Crumble into bits.

Drain and slice water chestnuts. Drain bean sprouts. Put both in bowl with spinach. Add crumbled bacon to bowl. Slice hard-boiled eggs into bowl.

Refrigerate.

Make dressing, mixing last 6 ingredients together (vinegar, oil, crushed garlic, salt, mustard, pepper). Beat with whisk or fork, in bowl, till well blended.

Just before serving, pour dressing over salad. Toss lightly 15 times till spinach is coated thoroughly but still cold and crisp.

+ +

PARTY #4 - PARTY #4 - PARTY #4 - PARTY #4 - PARTY #4 - PARTY #4 - PARTY #4 -

+ +

+ +
MENU (serves 4-6):   Bacon Spaghetti
                       Lettuce with Herb Salad Dressing
+ +

TIMING INFORMATION:

Spaghetti must be cooked at the last minute. However, the sauce can be made in advance - up to adding the bacon bits. Reheat, then add bacon.

Salad greens should be prepared in advance, in bowl; refrigerate. The dressing should be made well in advance for best flavor. Add it to greens and toss at the last minute.

+ BACON SPAGHETTI CHRIS AND ANDREA +   Takes 45 minutes

Serves 4-6. Described by Chris as "El Cheepo" and by Andrea as "our best, easy party," this great recipe is a Harvard favorite. Cook it only when bacon is on sale.

LINE UP YOUR INGREDIENTS:

1 lb. bacon	Salt and pepper
1 medium green pepper	Small (4 oz.) can mushroom bits
1 large onion	2 (8 oz.) cans tomato sauce
2 large cloves garlic	1 lb. thin spaghetti
3-4 stalks celery with leaves	½ bunch parsley
½ teaspoon oregano	Parmesan or Romano cheese, grated
½ teaspoon basil	

PREPARATION:

Use largest skillet. Cut up bacon. Fry over medium-high heat till crisp, not burned (6-8 minutes). Remove with slotted spoon to lots of paper towels to drain. Pour off most, not all, fat in skillet.

Remove seeds from green pepper. Slice thin. Peel onion. Chop up. Peel garlic. Chop up fine. Wash celery. Slice thin, leaves and all.

Sauté these vegetables in skillet over medium-high heat for 5 minutes, or till limp. Stir now and then.

Add oregano, basil, ½ teaspoon salt, and dashes of pepper. Drain mushroom bits. Add to skillet. Stir. Add cans of tomato sauce. Stir.

Cook on medium-low heat 15-20 minutes.

Meanwhile, boil spaghetti in largest (4-quart) pot, according to package instructions. Drain at sink in large strainer or colander.

Return spaghetti to pot. Pour sauce over it. Add bacon bits. Fold in till all is mixed.

With scissors, snip parsley on top. Serve. Dust each portion with grated cheese.

+ + + + + + + + + + + +

+ HERB SALAD DRESSING +

Makes 1 cup. Also known as Fines Herbes dressing, it's a simple, pepped-up version of traditional French dressing transformed with a few handy ingredients. This recipe makes enough for the party salad; or enough for 2-3 salads for 1-2 people during the working week. Refrigerate. It improves with age.

INGREDIENTS:

¼ teaspoon salt
¼ teaspoon pepper
¼ teaspoon Dijon (mild) mustard
¼ teaspoon basil (or thyme)
¼ cup red-wine vinegar

¾ cup salad oil (olive, corn)
2 teaspoons chopped fresh parsley (or 1 teaspoon dried)
1 garlic clove

In a small mixing bowl put salt, pepper, mustard, and basil. Mix together. Add vinegar. Stir well. Add olive oil and parsley. Whisk together till well mixed.

Pour into clean, dry 1-pint jar with cover. Peel garlic. Split in half. Drop into dressing. Cover. Refrigerate at least 3 hours.

Each time before using, shake up well.

+ + + + + + + + + + + +

+ +
MENU (serves 6-8):   Chicken Schizo
                        Carefree Oven Rice
                        Lettuce with Traditional French Dressing
+ +

TIMING INFORMATION:

Chicken Schizo may be assembled, even baked, in advance. If prebaked, reheat at 350 for 15 minutes, covered.

Rice can be made long before serving (convenient).

Salad: Assemble, chill, as long ahead as you want. Toss with dressing at the table. The recipe for the dressing is on page 31; double or triple. You can always use up the extra later. Greens should be well coated but not drowned.

+ CHICKEN SCHIZO +   Preparation: 10 minutes
                                         Cooking: 1 hour

Serves 8. This is where the frog turns into the prince. Three unlikely (ugh!) ingredients fuse, change character, and emerge triumphantly different. Terrific party recipe. Keep it to yourself as long as you can.

LINE UP YOUR INGREDIENTS:

Two 2½- or 3-lb. chicken fryers, cut up
8-oz. bottle Kraft Creamy French
      dressing

1-lb. can whole cranberry sauce
1 package Lipton's onion soup
Butter

PREPARATION:

Turn oven to 325.

Wash chicken pieces in cold tap water. Pat dry with paper towel.

Grease (with butter) a large 12″ × 18″ open roasting pan. (Or use two 9″ × 9″ square cake pans - a tight squeeze, but you can save out the bulky bony backs, necks, and gizzards. Freeze, and make soup of them, page 28.)

In largest mixing bowl, mix together thoroughly the French dressing, cranberries, and dry onion soup.

Dip pieces of chicken in sauce mixture to coat both sides well. Place in roasting pan. Pour sauce mixture over all. Cover pan with foil.

Place on center rack in oven. Bake at 325 for 45 minutes. Uncover pan. Bake 15 minutes more, uncovered.

+ <u>CAREFREE OVEN RICE</u> +

<u>Serves 6-8</u>. You need a casserole that can be put over direct heat. <u>Don't</u> use Pyrex.

INGREDIENTS:

4 tablespoons butter or margarine
2 cups rice (Uncle Ben's converted)

4 cups chicken broth (4 teaspoons
    chicken bouillon mix plus 4 cups
    <u>hot</u> water)

PREPARATION:

Turn oven to 350. Heat water in saucepan.

Cut up butter and melt in a 3-quart casserole. Don't brown it. Add rice. Stir till rice is opaque and coated with butter but not browned.

Add bouillon mix to hot water, stir. Add to rice and stir well.

Bake at 350, <u>uncovered</u>, for 45 minutes.

+ <u>COMMENT</u> +

This can be made ahead. To re-heat: Fluff rice with fork. <u>Cover</u> casserole. Heat at 350 for 10-15 minutes.

+ +

+ +

+ + + + + + + + + + + + + + + + + + + +
MENU (serves 6):   Marion's Pork Chop Dream
                       Mixed Salad Greens - Egg-
                       Mayonnaise Dressing
+ + + + + + + + + + + + + + + + + + + +

+ <u>MARION'S PORK CHOP DREAM</u> +   Preparation: 5 minutes
                                            Cooking: 40 minutes

<u>Serves 6</u>. Mix everything, even the rice, in the same skillet. A no-problem dish. It even makes its own gravy.

INGREDIENTS:

2 medium onions
2 tablespoons butter or margarine
6 (½" thick) center-cut pork chops
14½-oz. can Franco-American brown
    gravy

1 can water
4-oz. can sliced mushrooms
1 cup white rice (Uncle Ben's converted)
Salt

PREPARATION:

Peel and chop up onions. In large 12" skillet, heat butter over medium-high heat. Add onions. Cook and stir 2 minutes.

Add pork chops. Brown 3 minutes on each side.

Add brown gravy, water, mushrooms and juice, and white rice. Bring to a boil. Turn heat to <u>low</u>. Cover. Simmer, bubbling gently, 30 minutes. (Add ½ can water during cooking if rice appears too dry.)

Salt to taste, if necessary.

+ + + + + + + + + + + +

+ <u>MIXED SALAD GREENS -</u>   Takes 15 minutes
<u>EGG-MAYONNAISE DRESSING</u> +

<u>Serves 6</u>. As usual with salad, start the preparation before beginning dinner. In this case, just get the salad greens washed, dried, and refrigerated ahead of time. This salad turns out moist, a bit wilted but very good. The eggs make the dressing creamy.

INGREDIENTS:

1 small head iceberg lettuce, sliced thin
2 small heads Bibb lettuce (or Boston),
    washed and dried
1 small bunch watercress, stems
    removed

3 eggs
6 tablespoons mayonnaise (Hellmann's
    is best)
Salt and pepper

PREPARATION:

Slice up iceberg lettuce. Put in large bowl. Wash and dry Bibb or Boston lettuce, tear into bite-size pieces, and add to bowl. Remove stems of watercress. Cut up leaves into bowl.

Boil eggs 5 minutes only. Shell under cold tap water. Cut up onto lettuce. Stir in mayonnaise. Mix well. Add salt and pepper if necessary. Mix well again. Refrigerate till dinner. This is a delicious "wilted," rather than crunchy salad.

+ + + + + + + + + + + + + + + + + + + +

MENU (serves 6):   No-Problem Glazed Baked Ham
                   Grits Soufflé
                   Salad of your choice, maybe "George"

+ +

TIMING INFORMATION:

The Ham can be baked early in the day. (You'll have leftovers - one of the God-given principles of ham.)

The Grits Soufflé has a 10- to 15-minute waiting period after baking, or it can be made in advance. Reheat at 350 for 15 minutes.

Salad: Check the timing on the salad you select. All salads are made ahead.

+ NO-PROBLEM GLAZED BAKED HAM +   Takes 2½ hours

Serves 8-10. Since ham tastes just fine at room temperature, do this early in the day. Then your oven will be free later on to accommodate the perfect accompaniment, Grits Soufflé. This grand ham is moist and tender inside with a lovely sticky-sweet glaze outside. It turns out looking absolutely professional, yet is simplicity itself to do.

Buy a 4- to 5-lb. piece of precooked ham; ask for "end cut" or "shank cut."

Put ham on a rack in 13″ × 9″ roasting pan. Place it on center rack of a low (275) oven. Let it warm through for 2 hours. Take it out and let it cool 10 minutes while you make the glaze.

GLAZE INGREDIENTS:

1 tablespoon butter	Some fruit juice, beer, ginger ale
1½ cups brown sugar	(whichever you have around)
1 tablespoon dry mustard	10 whole cloves (optional; for
2 tablespoons flour	decoration)

PREPARATION:

Melt butter in a small saucepan over medium heat. Remove to counter. Stir in brown sugar, mustard, and flour. Mix well. Heat 2 minutes over low heat. Remove to counter.

Very gradually add the liquid in small quantities, about 1 teaspoon at a time. Stir after each addition. Do this until glaze has arrived at consistency of soft paste.

Now, score the ham: Cut diagonal gashes across top of fat, making diamond pattern. Insert a whole clove in center of each diamond (optional). Next, smear glaze all over top and along sides and both ends of ham.

Return ham to oven. Turn heat up to 350. Bake 30 minutes more.

+ <u>GRITS SOUFFLÉ</u> +

Preparation: 10 minutes
Cooking: 45 minutes

<u>Grits?</u>

Yep!

This soufflé is always served at Kentucky Derby parties and makes a believer out of any Yankee. By all means try it. (Do not let a Southerner catch you saying "hominy grits." However, this lovely stuff <u>is</u> hominy.) <u>Serves 6-8.</u>

LINE UP YOUR INGREDIENTS:

1 cup quick grits
2 cups milk
2 cups water
1 teaspoon salt
2 eggs

1 clove garlic
1 cup (8 oz.) shredded Cheddar cheese
1 stick (8 tablespoons) butter or
    margarine
½ cup light cream, or milk

PREPARATION:

You'll need a 3-quart casserole for this. Borrow one. Grease casserole.

In your largest saucepan, cook grits according to directions, BUT use half milk and half water plus the teaspoon of salt. When cooked, keep covered.

Crack and SEPARATE eggs. Put yolks in a cup and whites in a small mixing bowl.

Peel and mash or chop up garlic. Add to grits.

Shred cheese on large holes of grater. Add to grits.

Cut up butter in slices. Add to grits and bury deep, so it will melt.

With fork, lightly stir up egg yolks in cup. Add to the grits. With beater, beat whites till frothy.

Now, uncover grits. Stir around. Add milk (or cream) and stir. Add egg whites; gently fold in.

Pour all into greased casserole. Cook, covered, at 350 for 45 minutes. Remove.

Let it stand on counter, UNCOVERED, 10-15 minutes before serving so it won't be soupy. Don't worry. It won't get cold.

HOW TO CLEAN UP (page 15)

+ + + + + + + + + + + + + + + + + +

BREADS

BREAD IS SO EASY to make that it was one of the earliest foods concocted by man. Perhaps it was an accidental by-product of beer making; perhaps the reverse. It was made daily in every cave and castle.

There must be some common factor in our many inheritances having to do with bread, for the aroma of it baking in an oven pulls everybody like a magnet. Try Flash Beer Bread as a starter and see for yourself.

+ + + + + + + + + + + +

+ FLASH BEER BREAD +

Preparation: 3 minutes
Baking: 40 minutes

This tasty bread's big plus is the fact that it can be got together in a blink, no kneading, no punching, no waiting. Not a perfect sandwich bread, but it is wonderful for munching and toasting.

LINE UP YOUR INGREDIENTS:

3 cups SELF-RISING flour
3 tablespoons sugar

1 can beer
¼ cup (4 tablespoons) melted margarine

PREPARATION:

Turn oven to 350.
Mix together flour, sugar, and beer in mixing bowl. Stir batter to mix all well.
Grease a bread loaf pan. Pour in batter.
Bake on center rack of 350 oven for 30 minutes.
Melt margarine in small skillet. Remove bread from oven. Pour margarine over bread. Return bread to oven for 10 minutes more.
Leave on counter 5 minutes. Turn out onto rack. Let cool 15 minutes.

+ + + + + + + + + + + +

+ FAST SURVIVAL BREAD +

Preparation: 10 minutes
Baking: 1 hour and 10 minutes

There's no kneading or long waiting time with this recipe, and it makes one of the most delicious whole-wheat breads ever tasted.

LINE UP YOUR INGREDIENTS:

1½ cups whole-wheat flour
2 cups unbleached white flour
2 teaspoons baking soda

½ teaspoon salt
½ cup brown sugar
2 cups regular milk, or buttermilk

PREPARATION:

Turn oven to 350.
Grease a bread loaf pan (9" × 5").

Place a large sieve over a large mixing bowl. Measure into sieve the two kinds of flour, soda, and salt. Use a spoon to stir it until all of it drifts down into bowl.

Add the brown sugar and milk. Mix all THOROUGHLY so there are no air pockets. Pour into greased bread pan.

Put on center rack of oven. Bake at 350 for 1 hour plus 10 minutes. Remove to counter. Turn out of pan onto a rack.

Let bread rest 15 minutes before slicing. (Great spread with whipped sweet butter.)

+ + + + + + + + + + +

+ STEPHANIE'S PERFECT
BANANA BREAD +

Preparation: 15 minutes
Baking: 1 hour

This squishes together quickly and has a lovely flavor. The All-Bran gives it a sturdier quality than most banana breads. It is not gummy, nor does it collapse into crumbs.

LINE UP YOUR INGREDIENTS:

4-5 soft, overripe bananas
2 tablespoons water
1 teaspoon lemon juice
¼ cup melted butter or margarine
1 egg
½ cup sugar

1 cup Kellogg's All-Bran cereal
1½ cups flour (white, unbleached)
½ teaspoon salt
2½ teaspoons baking powder
½ teaspoon baking soda
4 oz. chopped walnuts or pecans (optional)

PREPARATION:

Turn oven to 350.

Grease a bread loaf pan (9" × 5").

In large mixing bowl, mash bananas with a fork till mushy, or put through a potato ricer, if you own one.

Add water and lemon juice and stir.

Melt butter in small pan till soft. Add to bowl and stir.

Beat egg slightly and add. Stir.

Add sugar and bran. Stir.

Place a large-size sieve over bowl. Measure in the flour, salt, baking powder, and soda. With a spoon, stir it around till all the dry ingredients sift into the bowl.

Mix everything together thoroughly, including nuts if you want, stirring only enough to dampen all ingredients. (In other words, don't beat it or get too vigorous.)

Put batter in a greased bread loaf pan. Put on center rack of oven. Bake for 1 hour.

Remove. Cool for 5 minutes. Gently turn out on a rack or wooden surface. Cool 10 minutes before slicing. Sheer bliss!

+ COMMENTS +

1. Stephanie says you could omit the nuts, but they're a nice crunchy surprise.

2. You can keep this moist for several days, wrapped and refrigerated.

+ + + + + + + + + + +

BIG MEAL SOUPS

IN JANUARY, WHEN WINTER seems to stretch ahead endlessly like a treeless tundra, when skies are bleak, when your professors seem increasingly unfriendly and your clothes too thin - there is no one thing quite as satisfying as hot, savory soups. They will warm and hearten you. The thought that they are there already made and waiting, like your favorite date, will revive you.

These are robust <u>big</u> meal soups in many ways: <u>Each is a complete meal</u> containing protein, vitamins, and minerals; <u>each will last for several days</u>. Take out the portion you need and heat it in a small pan. Each is famous in its own way and has its particular flavor.

At the chapter end there is a recipe for <u>Survival Bone Soup</u>. This predates Neanderthal days. Bones and throwaway scraps are cooked to extract all the vital essences. You may then use it, adding beans, etc., copying the earlier recipes, to produce your own, even-richer soup. Beans are used liberally in Big Meal Soups because they produce a gutsy flavor, they are available everywhere, and they are CHEAP.

+ + + + + + + + + + + +

+ <u>OLD-FASHIONED SPLIT PEA SOUP</u> +   Preparation: 5 minutes
Cooking: 2½ to 3 hours

<u>4-6 servings</u>. Age-old mainstay of the limited budget. Split pea soup is a valuable source of vitamins, minerals, and protein, and therefore gives you back far more than it costs. Long simmering produces the smooth, puréed quality.

INGREDIENTS:

1-lb. package dried split peas, rinsed in
    sieve
1-2 ham hocks
8 cups water

1 large onion
2 cloves garlic
1 teaspoon salt
4 all-beef frankfurters (optional)

PREPARATION:

In large (4-quart) soup pot put the split peas, ham hocks, and water.

Peel and chop up onion and garlic. (They disappear during cooking.) Add them to soup pot. Measure in salt.

Bring to a boil over <u>high</u> heat. Turn down to <u>low</u>. Cover pot, simmer 2½ hours, or till peas are tender. Stir occasionally.

Remove ham hocks. Cut meat off bone and cut meat into small pieces. Return meat to soup.

Taste with wooden spoon. Add more salt if necessary.

If you're adding frankfurters, slice them thin and add now. Simmer 10 more minutes. Serve with crusty bread.

+ COMMENT +

<u>Must</u> be made in a <u>heavy</u> pot to avoid burning bottom.

+ + + + + + + + + + + +

+ <u>LENTIL PEP-UP SOUP</u> +

Preparation: 10 minutes
Cooking: 2 to 2½ hours

<u>4-6 servings</u>. Lentils gained immortal fame via the biblical story of Esau's mess of pottage (lentils), for which he sold his birthright. Even back then they knew a good thing when they tasted it.

INGREDIENTS:

1-lb. package lentils, rinsed in sieve
1-lb. can peeled tomatoes and juice
7 cups water
½ lemon
1 large onion

1 teaspoon salt
½ teaspoon pepper
1 lb. kielbasas (Polish sausage), or white
    sausages (Bratwurst)

PREPARATION:

In large (4-quart) soup pot put lentils, tomatoes plus juice, and water.
Squeeze the ½ lemon into pot and then throw it in to cook with lentils.
Peel onion. Chop up. Add to pot, with salt and pepper.
Bring to a boil over <u>high</u> heat. Turn down to <u>low</u>. Cover. Simmer 2 hours, or till lentils are tender. Stir occasionally.
Slice kielbasas or sausages thin. Add to pot. Cook 15 minutes more.

+ COMMENTS +

1. This lentil soup can also be made completely different by simply following the ingredients for <u>Old-Fashioned Split Pea Soup</u>, just substituting lentils for the split peas.
2. <u>Must</u> be made in a <u>heavy</u> pot to avoid burning bottom.

+ + + + + + + + + + + +

+ <u>SEA FOOD CHOWDER</u> +

Preparation: 20 minutes
Cooking: 1 hour

<u>Serves 4-6</u>. A rich, briny concoction of fish, potatoes, herbs, and cream, this Boston-style chowder warms the cockles of your heart. (Will some med student please tell us the exact location of the cockles?)

INGREDIENTS:

¼ lb. bacon (or salt pork, rinsed and diced small)
3 medium potatoes
3 medium onions
1 large clove garlic
3 stalks celery and leaves
½ teaspoon thyme

2 cans clam juice
1 lb. thick fish fillets (cod, anglerfish, haddock)
Small bunch parsley
½ pint (1 cup) light cream or half-and-half
½ teaspoon salt
¼ teaspoon pepper

PREPARATION:

Peel and chop up potatoes in dice.
Peel and chop up onions and garlic.
Wash and slice across (1″ thick) the celery, plus leaves.
Cut fish into bite-size pieces. Extract any "hidden" bones.
Wash parsley. Shake off excess water. Discard stems. Chop up fine (or snip with scissors).
Cut bacon into ½″ strips. Fry it over medium-high heat in a 2- to 3-quart saucepan for 3-4 minutes, until somewhat browned. Stir now and then. Drain off about ½ the fat.
Add onions and garlic. Fry and stir for 2 minutes till onions are limp but not brown.
Add potatoes, celery, clam juice, ½ the parsley, thyme, and enough water to cover the vegetables.
Bring to a boil over high heat. Turn heat to low. Cover. Simmer 45 minutes.
Put in fish pieces. Cover. Simmer 15 minutes more. Remove from stove.
Add rest of parsley, salt, and pepper. Swirl in cream. Mix well.
Serve with oatmeal or whole-wheat toast, or warmed Sea Biscuits crackers.

+ COMMENTS +

1. When fish is on sale ("when," indeed!), it's interesting to try 2 or 3 varieties in the same chowder; buy ½ lb. of each.

2. If you find (dig up!) fresh chowder clams, you can use them (6 huge ones) instead of the fish. Open them by steaming in a tightly closed kettle containing ½″ of boiling water. Clams will open in 2-3 minutes. Cut them out of shell, and chop up into small pieces. Add them to the chowder only for the last 5 minutes of cooking. (Prolonged cooking turns clams into vulcanized rubber.)

Use the broth (water and clam juice) in which you steamed clams open: Pour broth into the saucepan containing onions and potatoes (be careful not to add sand and residue at bottom of broth kettle), and proceed as with recipe for Seafood Chowder. Now you have BOSTON CLAM CHOWDER!

3. Must be made in a heavy pot to avoid burning bottom.

+ + + + + + + + + + + +

+ <u>FIDEOS</u> +

Preparation: 20 minutes
Cooking: 30 minutes

<u>6 servings</u>. This is <u>Sopa Seca</u>, dry soup. The noodle nests come apart, absorbing all the liquid and flavor. You could eat it all day.

LINE UP YOUR INGREDIENTS:

2 medium onions
½ cup peanut oil
12-oz. box of <u>fideos</u> (noodle nests)
3 tomatoes

3 cups chicken broth (3 teaspoons
    instant chicken bouillon mix in 3
    cups hot water)
3 oz. grated Monterey Jack cheese

PREPARATION:

Peel and chop onions. Set aside.
In 12″ skillet, bring oil to hot over medium-high heat; takes 1-2 minutes.
Fry 3 <u>fideos</u> nests at a time till golden brown on both sides. Turn over with long-handled slotted spoon. (Don't let them burn!) Quickly scoop out <u>fideos</u> onto nearby plate.
Do this till all <u>fideos</u> are fried.
Turn onions into skillet. Fry 3-4 minutes, or till limp. Stir now and then.
Chop up tomatoes into bite-size chunks. Add to onions. Stir and cook 1-2 minutes.
Add <u>fideos</u> and chicken broth. Bring to boil on high heat. Turn down to low. Cover!
Cook till all liquid is absorbed, approximately 30 minutes. Serve in bowls, with grated cheese on top.

+ <u>COMMENT</u> +

<u>Must</u> be made in a <u>heavy</u> pot to avoid burning bottom.

+ + + + + + + + + + +

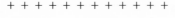

+ <u>LUCILE'S SAUSAGE-BEAN CHOWDER</u> +   Preparation: 5 minutes
                                           Cooking: 1 hour

<u>4-6 servings</u>. A real find! It's a terrific combination of sausage meat, beans, and other good things which tastes as though it's been simmering over a wood fire for days. Actual cooking time is 1 hour.

INGREDIENTS:

1 lb. bulk pork-sausage meat (or sweet Italian sausages, casings removed)	1 lb. can peeled tomatoes
1 medium onion	1 bay leaf
1 green pepper	1 tablespoon Worcestershire sauce
1 large clove garlic	2 medium potatoes
1 lb. can kidney beans	Salt to taste

PREPARATION:

In large (2- to 3-quart) saucepan, cook sausage over medium-high heat until all pink disappears. Break into bits with wooden spoon. Drain sausage well in sieve over grease can in sink. Leave 2 tablespoons fat in pan. Let sit while you chop onion, pepper, and garlic.

Pat sausage with paper towel to absorb as much grease as possible. Return to pot. Add garlic, onion, pepper. Cook, stirring now and then, till onion is limp (3-4 minutes).

Add kidney beans and juice, tomatoes and juice, bay leaf, and Worcestershire sauce. Bring to a bubble on <u>high</u> heat. Turn down to <u>low</u> heat. Cover. Simmer 30 minutes.

Meanwhile, peel potatoes and cut them into small dice. Add them to the chowder. Cover. Simmer 30 minutes more.

Remove bay leaf. Salt to taste. Serve with hot, crusty rolls and lots of sweet butter.

+ <u>COMMENT</u> +

<u>Must</u> be made in a <u>heavy</u> pot to avoid burning bottom.

+ + + + + + + + + + + +

+ <u>MINESTRONE MAGNIFICO</u> +   Preparation: 15 minutes
                                     Cooking: 45 minutes

<u>4-6 servings</u>. Everything marvelous is tossed into the pot in this Harold Coletta version of a famous Italian soup so thick you could almost eat it with a fork.

INGREDIENTS:

10-oz. package frozen chopped spinach
1 medium onion
2 cloves garlic
½ cup olive oil
1 large carrot
2 stalks celery and leaves
1-lb. head Savoy cabbage, or escarole
6-oz. can tomato paste
1 (10″) zucchini, or 2 small zucchini

Bunch parsley
1 teaspoon dried basil
1 teaspoon dried oregano
1 teaspoon salt
½ teaspoon pepper
2 cups chicken broth (2 teaspoons
    instant chicken bouillon mix plus
    2 cups hot water)
½ cup elbow macaroni, uncooked
1-lb., 4-oz. can cannellini (white kidney) beans

PREPARATION:

You need a heavy 4-quart pot for this one too.

Put spinach on counter to defrost.

Peel onion and garlic. Cut up. Scrape carrot. Remove root end. Slice thin. Wash celery. Slice into ½″ pieces, plus leaves.

Heat oil in the pot. Add onion, garlic, carrot, and celery. Cook on medium heat 5 minutes, stirring now and then.

Cut cabbage in quarters. Remove core and discard. Slice leaves into thin shreds.

Dilute tomato paste in ½ cup warm water. Add to the soup pot now.

Wash zucchini. Cut off ends. Slice in half, lengthwise. Then cut across, making ½″ slices.

Remove stems from ½ bunch of parsley. Chop up leaves.

Toss cabbage, zucchini, and parsley into soup pot. Stir around.

Add basil, oregano, salt, pepper, 2 cups chicken broth, and elbow macaroni. Stir around. Bring to a bubble over high heat. Turn down to low. Cover. Simmer 20 minutes.

Add cannellini beans, plus juice. Stir in. Cover. Cook, bubbling gently, 10 minutes more.

Bury defrosted spinach in center of soup. Cook till spinach is hot, stirring it through the soup. Serve in big bowls, steaming hot.

+ COMMENTS +

1. Harold says, "Great served with whole-wheat Italian bread and cheese, e molto vino!"

2. Reheat gently over low flame, and stir to bottom often. Thick stews and soups tend to have burned bottoms. (The heavier your pot, the safer your soup.)

+ + + + + + + + + + +

ACCORDING TO A SCRAP of manuscript dug up and recently deciphered by some Northwestern students: "Many years ago, the kingdom of Ecks was ruled by a mean, bowlegged king and his no-account, nearsighted wife. Selfish and greedy, they pampered themselves and their court, consuming gallons of rich cream soups, tons of fatty meats, and sensationally sweet, gloppy desserts by the cartload. They left nothing for their slaves but the calcium-rich bones, fish heads, chicken feet, and disdained green, leafy, vitamin-filled vegetables, all of which the wise old chef threw into an ever-simmering caldron.

Downstairs in the castle,
the slaves were a merry,
rosy-cheeked bunch . . .
+++++++++++++++

"Time passed in the castle. The nobles became obese and apathetic, with lackluster myopic eyes, zit-covered skin, and truly horrendous breath. Downstairs, the slaves were a merry, rosy-cheeked bunch, sleek of body, lustrous of hair, who capered around muscularly and laughed a lot, displaying rows of strong, flashing white teeth. . . ."

Here the manuscript breaks off. So we will never know how Ecks was rated. But the ancient message comes through loud and clear: "Castle slaves ate SURVIVAL BONE SOUP!"

+ SURVIVAL BONE SOUP +

In essence, this is compost soup. It's composed of leftovers, bones, scraps - most everything ordinarily destined for the garbage pail. It simmers away for hours and rewards you, in 1 serving, with the calcium equivalent of 3 quarts of milk!

PROCEDURE:

You'll need a 4-quart saucepan or soup kettle.

Put in 8 cups of water, leftover bones, 2 split fresh pigs' feet, 2 teaspoons salt, and ¼ cup vinegar. (Vinegar draws out the bones' precious calcium; you will neither taste nor smell it after cooking - it all disappears.) Add 1-2 cups fresh or leftover vegetables. Bring to a boil over high heat. Turn to low. Cover. Simmer 5 hours. Remove from stove. Leave as is, overnight, with lid partially off.

Next day, skim grease off top of cold broth with large spoon. At sink strain off broth through large strainer into big bowl.

You can eat this broth as is, now. Or, use it as a base for any soup you want to make: Chicken, bean, pea - you name it. Clearly, you'll get a far better, richer result than if you'd used plain tap water.

Pig's feet: Your butcher will think you are remarkable to ask for these. You don't really have to look at them; just shut eyes and put in pot. After cooking, they'll be just bones.

+ +

CRAM-ITS

+ +

YOU'RE DOWN TO THE WIRE. Your back is to the wall. You're in the pit with ravening wolves circling above and salivating heavily. In fact, it's Exam Week and you haven't much time.

CRAM-ITS are quick, filling, on-the-run foods with plenty of muscle. They'll tide you through the bleak week. And, they're great term-paper food, too. Stock up on the ingredients and eat when it suits you. Good luck!

+ + + + + + + + + + + +

+ <u>CHILI-IN-A-POCKET</u> +   Takes 15 minutes

<u>Serves 2</u>. This is fast to make, messy to eat. Worth it.

LINE UP YOUR INGREDIENTS:

1 medium onion   ¼ teaspoon oregano
1 garlic clove   ½ teaspoon salt
2 tablespoons oil (peanut, corn)   2 tablespoons ketchup
½ lb. ground beef (chuck)   Tabasco (2-3 dashes)
1 teaspoon chili powder   Pita bread
½ teaspoon cumin

PREPARATION:

Peel and chop onion and garlic.
Put oil in 8″ skillet over medium heat. Add beef, onion, and garlic. Fry 4-5 minutes.
Add everything. Cook 10 minutes, stirring now and then.
Warm pita bread in oven. Insert chili.

+ <u>COMMENT</u> +

You can put this between halves of split, heated rolls too.

+ <u>ONE-HANDED PIZZAS</u> +   Takes 10 minutes

<u>Serves 2.</u>

   LINE UP YOUR INGREDIENTS:

1 small can marinara sauce   4 slices Monterey Jack or provolone
2 English muffins   cheese

   PREPARATION:

   Warm sauce through in small pan.
   Toast muffins. Put on pie plate. Coat with sauce. Top with cheese.
   Broil, 7" from heat, till cheese melts. Watch it!

+ <u>COMMENTS</u> +

   1. If you brown <u>Italian sausage meat (4 links)</u> in a skillet 5 minutes till brown, then add some sauce and proceed as above, you'll have a mighty fine SAUSAGE PIZZA.
   2. Same goes for 6-8 mushrooms cooked in butter (5 minutes).
   3. And again, try 6 Jones sausages sliced up, fried, and mixed with some sauce. You almost can't lose this game.

+ + + + + + + + + + +

+ <u>FRENCH BREAD PIZZAS</u> +

<u>Serves 2-4.</u> An excellent substitute for the real thing, at a fraction of the cost. You can switch the ingredients to suit your mood or what's on hand and assemble the whole thing in a few minutes.
   Split <u>4 hero-size French loaves</u>. Put them on a 13" × 9" × 2" oven pan, split side up. Dribble <u>2 teaspoons oil</u> over each half. Use an <u>8-oz. can tomato sauce</u>: Smear 2-3 teaspoons tomato sauce over each half. Sprinkle ⅛ teaspoon <u>oregano</u> lightly over sauce. Cut up <u>4 oz. mozzarella cheese</u> (or Monterey Jack cheese), and dot all over each half. Seed and chop <u>1 green pepper</u>. Split, and chop up <u>3-4 scallions</u>, using both white and green parts. Mix scallions and peppers and arrange mixture over each half.
   Turn oven to "broil." Place oven rack 7" to 10" from heating element. Put oven pan in center of rack. Broil till cheese is melted, 1-2 minutes.

+ <u>COMMENTS</u> +

   1. For variety: Use 2 thin-sliced mushrooms on top, in place of green pepper and scallions. Or, try sliced black olives and chopped fresh tomatoes. Or, try very thin slices of pepperoni, alone or mixed with any of the chopped vegetables, as a topping.
   2. If you can't locate the hero-size loaves, cut a long French bread into 3 equal lengths and then split each of them in half. (Italian bread's a bit too thick around the middle, so it's unsatisfactory for this caper.)

+ KONGWICH +

Serves 2. One quick trip to the deli counter, and you assemble this yourself at home, saving time and dollars. Be sure you have on hand some ketchup (or chili sauce), some Hellmann's mayonnaise, butter, some iceberg lettuce, and 2 eggs, hard-boiled.

INGREDIENTS:

⅓ lb. sliced ham
⅓ lb. sliced turkey breast
⅓ lb. sliced roast beef (optional; it may
    be $100 a lb.)

⅓ lb. sliced Swiss or provolone cheese
1 loaf Italian bread, or 4 hard rolls

PREPARATION:

Hard-boil 2 eggs (15 minutes).
Mix together 4 tablespoons ketchup and 4 tablespoons of mayonnaise in a small bowl. (Russian dressing, sort of.)
Peel and chop up eggs. Add to bowl. Stir around.
Split the bread. Butter it on both sides.
Add the sliced meats. Cover thickly with the Russian dressing.
Add sliced cheese. Add a couple of lettuce leaves, cut up.
Cover with other half of bread. Cut in 2 portions. A big meal: a Kongwich!

+ + + + + + + + + + +

+ GOOD GUY'S WESTERN SANDWICH +   Takes 15 minutes

Serves 2. Vic, a good guy from Columbia U., Class of '17, suggested this omelet you can eat plain or as a sandwich. Thanks!

LINE UP YOUR INGREDIENTS:

1-2 slices bacon
1 medium onion
1 small green pepper

2 eggs
1 tablespoon milk
Bread and mayonnaise, or butter

PREPARATION:

Cut up bacon. Fry in 8″ skillet on medium-high heat 2-3 minutes.
Peel and chop onion. Chop green pepper; discard stem and seeds.
In mixing bowl, beat eggs and milk well. Add salt.

Put onion and pepper in skillet. Fry 3-4 minutes with bacon, medium heat, till onion wilts.

Pour in beaten eggs. Stir a bit to mix. Turn to low heat. Cover pan. Cook 3 minutes. Shake pan now and then.

Uncover. Flip over. Cook 2 minutes. Cut in half.

Meanwhile you've toasted bread, 4 slices. Smear with mayonnaise or butter.

Makes 2 sandwiches.

+ + + + + + + + + + + +

+ HOT TORPEDO +

Serves 2-4.

Turn your oven to 500. Split 4 hero loaves.

Mash 2 cloves peeled garlic (use garlic press) onto a shallow dish. Add 4 tablespoons soft butter. Mash garlic and butter together thoroughly with a dinner fork or back of a wooden spoon.

Put each hero on a piece of foil large enough to encase. Spread split sides with garlic butter.

Add to each torpedo: 4 slices mozzarella cheese, 4 slices provolone cheese, and 4 slices boiled ham. Put the ham between the 2 cheeses. Cover with other halves of loaves.

Wrap tightly in foil. Place on an ovenproof pan. Bake at 500, for 15 minutes.

Remove. Let cool a minute. Unwrap torpedoes, and go!

+ + + + + + + + + + + +

+ SALAD FOR PITA BREAD +

INGREDIENTS:

3 slices bacon (optional)
1 ripe avocado
1 tablespoon lemon juice
1 medium tomato
3-4 scallions

2 tablespoons olive oil
½ teaspoon salt
1 cup sprouts (soybean or alfalfa)
6 small-size pitas

PREPARATION:

In 8" skillet, fry the bacon crisp. Drain on paper towel. Crumble it and set aside.

Peel avocado. Discard pit. Slice into large mixing bowl. Pour lemon juice over avocado.

Chop up tomato. Add that.

Remove root end of scallions. Slice up whites and two-thirds of greens. Add to bowl.

Pour in olive oil, salt, sprouts, and crumbled bacon. Gently toss this salad till well mixed.

Warm the pitas in oven. Fill with the salad.

+ TABOULEH +

Pronounced Ta-boó-lee. This makes a several-day supply for 2 people. It's filling, riddled with vitamins A, B, and C, and its nutty wheat flavor is unique.

LINE UP YOUR INGREDIENTS:

3 cups boiling water
1 cup bulgur wheat
1 bunch (4-6) scallions
2 bunches parsley
3 large tomatoes
4 stalks celery, with leaves

½ cup (4 oz.) olive oil
Juice of large lemon (4 tablespoons)
1 teaspoon salt
1 teaspoon sesame oil (optional)
Some lettuce, romaine or anything
   crunchy; or pita bread

PREPARATION:

In saucepan, bring water to a boil.

Into large mixing bowl, measure bulgur wheat. Add boiling water. Cover bowl. Put aside to set for 45 minutes.

Remove scallion root ends. Chop up whites and the greens halfway to ends.

Rinse parsley under cold-water tap. Shake dry. Chop leaves, or snip with scissors.

Chop up tomatoes.

Wash and chop celery stalks and leaves.

When bulgur wheat has soaked for 45 minutes, drain well in sieve at sink. Add all ingredients: olive oil, lemon juice, scallions, parsley, tomatoes, celery, salt, and sesame oil. Mix thoroughly.

Let this set again for several hours. Flavors mingle.

Serve on lettuce leaves. Or, eat wrapped in lettuce leaves. And good too inside warmed pita bread.

Cover and refrigerate remainder for later snacking.

+ COMMENTS +

1. You might consider adding 2-3 chopped hard-boiled eggs once in a while. Or, some chopped fresh mint leaves, when available. (Grow your own plant on your sunniest windowsill. Hardy like a weed.

2. Jonathan says, "An addition of a peeled, seeded, chopped cucumber is a great on-the-spot idea, but don't let the cucumber stay mixed in the main bowl for long. The tabouleh gets soggy."

3. Clearly this dish is best made in summer when vegetables, like tomatoes, are more plentiful, cheaper, and have more flavor.

+ + + + + + + + + + +

SUMMER SESSION

WHEN IT'S HOT AND steamy in the dorm, and the air conditioner's broken down, and you're perspiring all over the term paper; when someone suggests a picnic in the park and asks you to "bring something"; when you want to show off with a casual repertoire of summer foods: Here are icy soups, full-meal salads, plus a tropical curry, even a cold, uncooked spaghetti sauce. Beat the heat! (Take Oceanography.)

+ + + + + + + + + + + +

+ <u>VICHYSSOISE</u> +   Takes 20 minutes
                                          Chill 1 hour, or more

<u>Serves 2</u>. Of international fame. A lovely creamy soup which can be made well ahead, except for final addition of cream. Social note: Vichyssoise is pronounced "Vishee- swazz," <u>not</u> "Veeshee-swa." You'll need a blender. Really POST GRADUATE cooking, but easy.

INGREDIENTS:

2 medium potatoes (½ lb.)
2 leeks
1 medium onion
1 clove garlic
2 tablespoons oil (corn)

2 cups chicken broth (2 teaspoons
     instant chicken bouillon mix in 2
     cups hot water)
½ teaspoon salt
½ cup light cream or half-and-half
Chives, or green tops of 2 scallions

PREPARATION:

Peel and cut up potatoes. Cook them in 2-quart saucepan, in water to cover, until soft (15 minutes).

Remove root end of leeks. Slice white part thin. (Beware! When you get near the green part, there's hidden dirt. Wash well.) Use all the whites and 2-3 inches of green tops. (Discard remainder.)

Peel and chop up onion and garlic.

In 8" skillet, heat oil. Add leeks, onions, and garlic. Cook, stirring, over medium heat 3-4 minutes. Cover. Turn to low heat. Cook 5 minutes till wilted but <u>not</u> brown.

Drain potatoes into sieve over sink. Return them to saucepan. Leave on counter.

Add onion-leek mixture from skillet to saucepan.

Measure in the chicken broth and salt. Stir to mix.

Using a soup ladle, or largest spoon, pour ½ the mixture into blender container. Run blender (<u>covered</u>) on high till all liquefies. Pour off into large mixing bowl or pitcher.

Repeat till everything is well blended.

Chill the soup an hour or more.

Just before serving, stir in cream and mix thoroughly.

Top with 2-3 tablespoons chopped chives, if you can find them <u>FRESH</u> or the chopped green part of 2-3 scallions.

+ <u>COMMENTS</u> +

    1. This soup is good in the winter too. Serve <u>hot</u>.
    2. If you can't find leeks, use an additional medium-size onion.
    3. Impressive soup to serve to a date.

+ + + + + + + + + + +

+ <u>GAZPACHO</u> +   Takes 10 minutes

<u>Serves 4</u>. Spicy, sophisticated. This cold soup is easy (a liquid salad). You will feel honorably full of vitamins.

INGREDIENTS:

Two 12-oz. cans V-8 juice	1 avocado
2 cucumbers	4 scallions
1 green pepper	2 tomatoes

PREPARATION:

Pour V-8 juice into a 2-quart jar.
Peel cucumbers. Cut in half, lengthwise. Run spoon along centers to remove seeds. Chop up. Seed and chop up green pepper. Add cukes and pepper to juice.
Peel avocado. Remove pit. Dice up small. Add to juice.
Remove root ends of scallions. Chop up white and greens. Add to juice.
Cut up tomatoes in small chunks. Add to juice. Stir.
Let stand in refrigerator 1 hour, or more, till gazpacho becomes icy cold.

+ <u>COMMENT</u> +

To ripen an avocado on-the-spot, see page 89.

+ + + + + + + + + + +

+ <u>ICY CREAM OF CUCUMBER SOUP</u> +   Takes 10 minutes
                                         Chill 1 hour

<u>Serves 4</u>. A sensational pickup served on a hot sandy beach in July. Keep it in a Thermos. (This soup also merits special consideration as a hangover remedy.) You need a blender.

INGREDIENTS:

2 long cucumbers
4 scallions
½ teaspoon salt
2 cups chicken broth (2 teaspoons
    instant chicken bouillon mix plus
    2 cups hot water)

2 tablespoons fresh dill, or 1 tablespoon
    dried dillweed
½ cup sour cream (4 oz.)

PREPARATION:

Peel cucumbers. Slice in half, lengthwise. Use a teaspoon to run along centers, removing seeds. Then cut up cucumbers and drop into blender container.

Remove root end of scallions. Slice up, using whites and half the greens. Add to container.

Measure in salt, chicken broth, and chopped-up (or dried) dill.

Turn on blender (covered) to high speed. When almost liquefied but still a little lumpy turn off blender.

Chill in refrigerator 1 hour or more.

When serving, mix well with sour cream, a bit at a time, in a mixing bowl. Then pour into cups. This avoids lumps of cream.

When it's hot and steamy
in the dorm . . .
. . . try COLD spaghetti
sauce (page 131)
+ + + + + + + + + + + + + + +

+ <u>JUANAVEETCH</u> +

Preparation: 15 minutes
Cooking: 15 minutes

Also spelled "Won-uv-itch," and "Ooo-on-uv-eech." The name makes the recipe easy to remember. It's a cold soup.

INGREDIENTS:

1 small onion
1 large apple
   (Delicious, Granny Smith)
1 large potato
1 medium banana
1 rib celery plus leaves

1 pint chicken broth (use 2 teaspoons
     instant chicken bouillon mix plus
     2 cups hot water)
1 teaspoon curry powder
½ teaspoon salt
1 tablespoon butter
1 cup light cream

PREPARATION:

Peel and cut up the onion, apple, and potato. Put them in blender.

Peel banana. Slice it into blender.

Wash celery. Peel with vegetable peeler; strings don't blend. Slice stalk and leaves into blender.

Add 1 cup of chicken broth. <u>Cover</u> blender.

Run blender on high speed till vegetables and fruit liquefy. Pour blender contents into 2-quart saucepan.

Add other half (2nd cup) of chicken broth to soup mixture. Stir to mix.

Bring to a boil over high heat. QUICKLY turn heat to low. Cover. Simmer 15 minutes. Remove to counter.

Put 2-3 tablespoons of the soup in a cup. Add the curry powder. Stir till well mixed. Add that back to the saucepan, add salt, add the butter (cut up to melt faster). Stir till butter melts. Let cool to tepid.

Add cream. Refrigerate at least 1 hour.

+ + + + + + + + + + +

+ <u>6-MINUTE COLD-COOKED CHICKEN</u> +

This is an ancient Chinese secret method, using only 6 minutes of heat. There's a catch, of course; there always is: You <u>must</u> start your chicken 3-4 hours ahead of time. But if you do, you'll have <u>the world's tenderest chicken</u>, juicy and full of flavor. Plus that, your kitchen will be cool and steam-free.

INGREDIENTS:

2½- to 3-lb. chicken fryer, whole or cut up

Enough cold water to cover the chicken by 3 inches

PREPARATION:

You'll need a deep soup kettle for this one.

Remove innards (heart, liver, gizzard, neck). Set aside to freeze later on.

Put chicken in kettle. Cover with COLD water.

Bring to a boil over high heat. Boil, on high, for 6 minutes. Remove kettle to counter. Cover tightly with lid. Go away and do many things for 3 hours.

When you return, lift out chicken onto a large dish. You are now ready to make salad, sandwiches, or a quickie casserole (see page 147) with your cooked chicken.

+ COMMENTS +

1. Unlike other boiled chicken recipes, this method causes the flavor to implode, hence the chicken is marvelous, but no chicken soup evolves. All the goodness remains in the chicken. Discard the water, or use it to make soup of whatever frozen chicken innards you have on hand (page 28).

2. Fry the liver for breakfast: 2½ minutes in 1 teaspoon butter in small skillet, medium heat.

+ + + + + + + + + + +

+ 4 SUMMA CUM LAUDE SALADS +

On a hot, steamy day, any one of these cold salads served with warmed, crusty rolls (or as sandwiches on toasted bread) is all you'll need. Be frugal; use leftovers. Or, be enterprising; start from scratch. Most of the ingredients are interchangeable, with occasional exceptions. Believe it, when temperatures soar to 90, salad's the only way to go.

+ + + + + + + + + + +

1. + WHOLE WORLD EGG SALAD +

Serves 2. If the whole world started with an egg, you can too.

4-5 hard-boiled eggs, peeled and chopped up

3 scallions (green onions), chopped up

2 stalks of celery and leaves, washed and chopped up

1 small green pepper (optional), seeded and chopped up

½ teaspoon imported mustard (Dijon)

3-4 tablespoons mayonnaise (Hellmann's is best)

Salt to taste

Small head of lettuce (romaine, Boston, Bibb)

Put eggs, scallions, celery, green pepper, mustard, and mayonnaise in a mixing bowl. Stir to mix well. Salt lightly to taste.

Wash and dry lettuce leaves. Spoon egg salad on top.

+ + + + + + + + + + +

2. + CHUNKY-STYLE HAM SALAD +

Serves 2. At your local deli, ham salad is usually a ground-up, baby food-textured mess of who knows what's in it. This one's chewy and full of flavor.

½ lb. boiled ham unsliced (or 1¼ cups your own leftover roast ham), cut up into small dice
3 stalks celery, washed and chopped up
1 small green pepper, seeded and chopped up

1 small onion, peeled and chopped fine
3 tablespoons Hellmann's mayonnaise
Small head green lettuce (romaine, Boston)

Mix everything together in a large bowl. Add a tiny bit of salt and pepper, if necessary. Serve on lettuce leaves, washed and dried.

+ + + + + + + + + + +

3. + CHICKEN (TURKEY) SALAD +

Serves 2. Be sure to use the vinegar. It adds a necessary, snappy touch.

½ lb. thick-sliced cooked breast of chicken or turkey, chopped up (1½ cups); see pages 121-122 for cooked chicken
3 stalks celery and leaves, washed and chopped up
3 scallions, roots removed. Slice white and greens, and chop

3 tablespoons parsley, washed, dried, and chopped up
3 tablespoons Hellmann's mayonnaise
½ teaspoon wine vinegar
Salt and pepper to taste
1 small head green leafy lettuce

Mix everything together. Serve on bed of lettuce.

+ + + + + + + + + + +

4. + SALMON SALAD CUM LAUDE +

Serves 2. Step right up and get your brain food here, folks. Your low-calorie minerals too. Fish is the thing. Substitute tuna, if that's your preference.

1 medium (7¾ oz.) can salmon or tuna, drained

2 hard-boiled (15 minutes) eggs, peeled and quartered

3 scallions, root ends removed. Slice up white and ¾ green part, and chop

3 stalks celery and leaves, washed and chopped up

4 tablespoons Hellmann's mayonnaise

1 large tomato, sliced (optional)

Small head green leafy lettuce

Directions here are ambivalent: If you're making straight salad to go onto lettuce leaves, don't mix in the eggs. Leave the eggs quartered and use them as garnish placed around the salad, with sliced tomato.

If you're making this as a sandwich filler, chop up the peeled eggs and incorporate them into the other ingredients in a mixing bowl. Salt is not usually necessary here.

+ COMMENTS +

1. For variety: Buy a ripe avocado. Cut it open. Remove pit. Stuff avocado with any of the above creamy salads. (Some people successfully grow pretty plants from the pit.)

2. It's summer. Tomatoes are at their peak. Buy big ones. Slice off top. Scoop out middle. Stuff with one of the above salads.

+ + + + + + + + + + + +

+ 2 HONOR ROLL TUNA SALADS +

These are both real meal-on-the-plate salads, not to be confused with the sandwich-filler varieties. One is an original, the other an international favorite. Take your pick. It's a long hot summer. Pick both.

+ + + + + + + + + + + +

1. + ORIGINAL TUNA SALAD BERNADETTE +

Serves 2-4. This is a make-ahead meal. So leave time (1 hour) for things to cool down and get together in the refrigerator.

INGREDIENTS:

1 small (1-lb.) head red cabbage

1 medium red onion

2 stalks celery and leaves

1 small clove garlic

1 medium (9¼ oz.) can tuna

⅓ cup olive oil

1 tablespoon wine vinegar

½ teaspoon salt

PREPARATION:

Split and quarter red cabbage. Remove core; discard. Chop up cabbage in bite-size pieces.

Put in saucepan with enough water to cover. Bring to a boil over <u>high</u> heat. Turn down to <u>medium.</u> Cook 20 minutes. Drain at sink into strainer.

Meanwhile: Peel and chop red onion.

Wash and slice celery and leaves thin.

Peel and mash garlic.

In large bowl put tuna, drained, plus the cooked cabbage, the onion, celery, garlic, and salt.

Pour in olive oil and vinegar. Mix well. Refrigerate, covered, 1 hour or more.

Serve with hot Italian bread spread with sweet butter. A feast!

+ + + + + + + + + + + +

2. + <u>TUNA AND VEGETABLE SALAD</u> +

<u>Serves 2-4</u>. Known the world over as <u>Salade Niçoise</u> this short-cut version (using canned things) is as appealing to the eye as to the appetite. It should be served icy cold.

INGREDIENTS:

2 eggs	3 medium tomatoes
1-lb. can whole, or sliced, potatoes	1 clove garlic
1-lb. can green beans	Vinegar (wine)
1 medium (9¼ oz.) can white solid-pack tuna	Oil (olive)
	Salt and pepper
1 tin rolled anchovy fillets (optional)	<u>Dijon</u> mustard
Small (3½ oz.) can pitted black olives	Lettuce

PREPARATION:

Hard-boil eggs 15 minutes. Crack and peel under cold tap water. Dry off.

While eggs are cooking: Open and drain potatoes. Slice them into a small mixing bowl.

In a cup mix together: garlic, peeled and mashed; 1 tablespoon vinegar, 3 tablespoons olive oil, ¼ teaspoon each salt and pepper, ½ teaspoon mustard. Stir rapidly with a fork, and then pour the dressing over sliced potatoes. Mix gently to coat all. Set aside to marinate.

On a large serving dish or platter, arrange lettuce leaves (2 or more per person), covering bottom of plate.

Drain green beans. Arrange at one end of platter.

Drain tuna. Arrange at center of platter.

Drain anchovy fillets and olives. Quarter tomatoes and eggs.

Put sliced potatoes at other end of platter, with anchovy fillets on top (not the whole tin; too much salt).

Surround tuna with olives.

Make a second batch of dressing, <u>doubling</u> the vinegar, oil, and mustard, but NOT the salt and pepper. (Omit the garlic here.) Mix together.

Dribble dressing over green beans and tuna.

Garnish platter with quartered tomatoes and eggs.

Refrigerate about 30 minutes. Serve with warm, crusty rolls and sweet butter.

+ + + + + + + + + + + +

+ <u>3-BEAN SALAD</u> +

<u>Serves 6-8</u>. A different, tasty side dish for a crowd. Good with franks or kielbasas (Polish sausage). Excellent alongside thick slices of ham. (Or, if you want to make it a whole meal in one bowl, you can cut the meat into chunks and incorporate it right into the 3-Bean mixture.) Invigorating too is the addition of a zippy French dressing.

INGREDIENTS:

¼ teaspoon salt
⅛ teaspoon pepper
1 clove garlic
½ teaspoon mustard (Dijon)
1 tablespoon lemon juice
¼ cup oil (salad or olive)

1 can chick-peas (garbanzos)
1 can white beans (cannellini)
1 can Chinese bean sprouts
1 large red onion
1 large green pepper
Head of lettuce (romaine, Boston, Salad Bowl)

PREPARATION:

Use a large mixing bowl.

Make the French dressing first. Put salt and pepper in the bowl. Peel garlic clove. Cut it up into bowl. With the back of a wooden spoon, mash garlic well into the salt till it's entirely mushy.

Add mustard and lemon juice. Stir.

Add oil. Beat with a fork or whisk till well mixed.

Open the 3 cans of beans, drain them at sink. Put the bean sprouts in a strainer, and run cold tap water over them thoroughly to refresh them. Shake dry in a towel.

Add all beans to mixing bowl.

Peel and chop red onion. Add it.

Slice open green pepper. Remove stem and seeds. Chop up. Add to bowl.

Mix and stir everything together thoroughly. Refrigerate 30 minutes.

Serve on washed and dried lettuce leaves.

+ + + + + + + + + + + +

+ <u>CHEF SALAD</u> +

<u>Serves 2-4</u>. This whole-meal salad is a breeze to prepare because the man behind the deli

counter does most of the cutting work. Then you, like the master artisan you are, assemble the slivered cheese and meats into a grande finale masterpiece, bathed with Creamy Italian Dressing.

INGREDIENTS:

2 eggs
2 medium tomatoes
⅓ lb. sliced boiled or baked ham
⅓ lb. sliced turkey or chicken breast
⅓ lb. sliced roast beef (optional; check
     price)
⅓ lb. sliced Swiss cheese
Small (4-oz.) can black <u>pitted</u> olives

Small head green leafy lettuce (romaine,
     Bibb, Boston)
½ teaspoon salt
¼ teaspoon pepper
1 clove garlic
1 tablespoon mayonnaise (Hellmann's)
1 tablespoon wine vinegar or lemon juice
¼ cup salad oil (olive, corn)

PREPARATION:

Hard-boil eggs for 15 minutes. Peel under cold tap water. Quarter and set aside.
Quarter tomatoes. Set aside.
Stack sliced meats, and cut into thin strips about 2"-3" long.
Sliver Swiss cheese the same way.
Drain olives. Wash and dry lettuce.
Make salad dressing.

+ + + + + + + + + + +

+ <u>CREAMY ITALIAN DRESSING</u> +

Into a large bowl, large enough to accommodate the above meats and cheese, sprinkle salt and pepper.

Peel garlic clove. Cut it up into slices and put in the bowl. With the back of a wooden spoon, mash the garlic into the salt and pepper till it's all pulpy.

Add mayonnaise and mash together some more.

Add vinegar and olive oil. Beat vigorously with a fork or whisk till the dressing is creamy and smooth.

Add the meats and cheese to the dressing and stir to coat everything.

Tuck lettuce leaves (2-3 per person) halfway down around sides of bowl; let top half of lettuce leaves stand up like a collar.

Sprinkle olives on top. Garnish with wedges of tomato and egg.

+ + + + + + + + + + +

+ <u>THOUSAND ISLAND SALAD DRESSING</u> +   Takes 15 minutes in all

Make this before you start cooking dinner as it <u>isn't</u> something you can splash together at the end. What it <u>is</u> is one of the most savory, creamy salad dressings invented. A treat on really crisp-type lettuce like <u>iceberg</u> or <u>romaine</u>.

INGREDIENTS:

1 egg, hard-boiled
1 small (golf-ball size) onion
3 tablespoons chili sauce or ketchup

1 cup Hellmann's mayonnaise
Salt and pepper

PREPARATION:

Hard-boil the egg (15 minutes).
Peel and chop onion fine. Put it in small bowl.
Shell egg under cold-water tap. Dry. Chop up fine into bowl. Add chili sauce and mayonnaise. Mix together. Taste before adding salt and pepper. Refrigerate.
Serve on lettuce which is finely slivered (6-8 leaves romaine, washed and dried; or ½ small head iceberg lettuce).

+ + + + + + + + + + + +

+ <u>2 ALL-TIME FAVORITES</u> +

No American summer session would be complete without once eating a meal of franks, or ham, and <u>Potato Salad</u>. Its popular twin, <u>Macaroni Salad</u>, is equally soul-satisfying, and goes along happily with hamburgers too. Here they are:

+ <u>POTATO SALAD</u> +

<u>Serves 2-4</u>. You make this salad in the morning, or hours ahead, and refrigerate.

INGREDIENTS:

4 medium (tennis-ball size) potatoes
2 eggs, hard-boiled
1 small (golf ball) onion
1 sour pickle (3″ long)

¼ cup (4 tablespoons) Hellmann's
    mayonnaise
1 teaspoon mild mustard
½ teaspoon salt

PREPARATION:

Boil potatoes 20-30 minutes, till fork-tender. Peel. Cut into bite-size chunks. Cool in refrigerator.
Hard-boil eggs, 15 minutes. Shell under cold tap water. Cool in refrigerator.
Chop up eggs. Peel and finely chop onion. Chop up pickle.

In a small bowl: Mix together mayonnaise, mustard, and salt.

In large bowl, put everything. Mix together gently (so potatoes won't get bashed about too much). Add a little extra mayonnaise, if you prefer a creamier salad.

You can serve this on lettuce, or not, as you wish.

+ MACARONI SALAD +

Serves 2-4. Another make-ahead salad. Plan to leave a couple of hours between making and serving it.

INGREDIENTS:

2 cups elbow macaroni
2 teaspoons salad oil
1 small (3½ oz.) jar sliced pimentos

1 small green pepper
⅓ cup Hellmann's mayonnaise
½ teaspoon salt

PREPARATION:

Cook macaroni according to package instructions. Drain into sieve at sink. Run cold tap water over it to cool it and to prevent its sticking together.

Put macaroni in a large mixing bowl. Measure in the salad oil and stir well to coat macaroni; also prevents sticking together.

Drain pimentos. Chop up in small bits. Add to bowl.

Halve green pepper. Remove stem and seeds. Chop up fine. Add to bowl.

Stir in mayonnaise and salt. Mix well. Refrigerate no less than 1 hour before serving.

+ + + + + + + + + + +

+ MIP'S SUMMER BOUNTY BOUQUET +   Preparation: 15 minutes
                                         Steaming: 45 minutes

Serves 6. People with their own vegetable gardens often concoct "ratatouille." This is a substance which looks, and often tastes, as though it has been trodden on by the entire football team. Here, the same vegetables retain their colorful identities and tastes.

INGREDIENTS:

2 medium onions
2 large cloves garlic
4 tablespoons oil (olive or corn)
1 large green pepper
1-lb. eggplant

3 small zucchini (or yellow summer
    squash)
3 ripe medium-size tomatoes
Small bunch fresh basil (2 tablespoons
    dried)
1 teaspoon salt

PREPARATION:

Peel and chop onions and garlic cloves.

Put them in large 12″ skillet over medium-low, with the oil. Let them cook gently.

Split green pepper. Remove seeds and stem end. Slice up. Add to skillet. Turn up heat to medium. Stir occasionally.

Meanwhile: Slice top and end off eggplant. Don't peel. Slice 1″ thick across. Cut slices up into large cubes. Layer on top of green pepper in skillet.

Wash zucchini. Trim off ends. Slice 1″ thick, and add on top of eggplant.

Slice and chop up tomatoes in large chunks. Layer on top of zucchini.

Remove stems of basil. Toss basil leaves over tomatoes.

Sprinkle salt over all.

Cover <u>tightly</u>. Steam on medium-low for 45 minutes. Serve at once.

+ COMMENT +

If the lid isn't too great a fit, use aluminum foil first, then the lid, to make as air-tight a cover as possible. Don't peek during cooking time. The vegetables must cook gently in the accumulated steam.

+ + + + + + + + + + +

+ HEAT-WAVE CHICKEN CURRY +

Preparation: 10 minutes
Cooking: 15 minutes

<u>Serves 2-4</u>. Tradition has it that, in torrid climates, ingesting hot spicy food is somehow cooling to the brow. As examples we recall those stinging chilies of Mexico, steamy Indian curries, and the peppery, spiced dishes of Africa. Could they know something we don't? Another tradition is that almost any leftover diced meat can be curried. True.

INGREDIENTS:

2 cups diced cooked chicken (1 lb.)
1 large onion
1 large clove garlic
3 tablespoons butter or margarine
1 tablespoon flour
2 teaspoons curry powder

1 cup chicken broth (use 1 teaspoon
    instant chicken bouillon mix in 1
    cup hot water)
2-3 dashes Tabasco sauce (optional)
Small bunch coriander or parsley, fresh
¼ teaspoon salt

PREPARATION:

Cut up chicken into bite-size pieces.

Peel and chop onion and garlic.

In 2-quart saucepan, melt butter over medium-high heat. Add onion and garlic. Cook and stir 3-4 minutes till onion is limp but not browned.

Remove pan from heat. Stir in flour and curry powder. Stir to make a paste.

Return to heat. Slowly add chicken broth (⅓ cup at a time), and stir constantly so sauce won't lump. Cook on medium-low 3-4 minutes, or till sauce thickens.

Add chicken and Tabasco sauce. Stir. Cover. Turn heat to <u>low</u>. Cook 10 minutes.

Chop up 3 tablespoons coriander or parsley.

Serve curry on <u>RICE</u> (page 42).

Sprinkle top of curry with chopped coriander for extra color and mysterious exotic flavor.

+ <u>COMMENTS</u> +

1. If you have no leftover chicken, make some; see pages 121-122.

2. Leftover lamb or seafood is a fine substitute for the chicken. Also turkey (roast; in cold weather).

+ + + + + + + + + + + +

+ <u>SPAGHETTI WITH COLD SAUCE</u> +   Takes 15 minutes

<u>Serves 4</u>. This avoids long, hot sauce-making in summer. Fresh, <u>cold</u> blended vegetables go over the hot spaghetti.

INGREDIENTS:

4 ripe tomatoes	⅓ cup oil (olive is best here), and 2
2 large cloves garlic	more tablespoons at end
½ cup (small bunch) fresh basil	½ teaspoon salt
½ bunch fresh parsley	1 lb. <u>thin</u> spaghetti (spaghettini)

PREPARATION:

Cut up tomatoes. Put them in blender container.

Peel and cut garlic in half. Add to container.

Remove stems from basil, and parsley. Add to container.

Next add olive oil and salt.

Run blender (<u>covered</u>) until vegetables are thoroughly chopped up.

Cook spaghetti according to package directions. Drain it at sink into sieve. Put it in large bowl. Add 2 tablespoons more of olive oil and toss thoroughly.

Now quickly add the sauce, toss the sauce through the spaghetti at the table, and serve.

+ + + + + + + + + + +

+ CORN ON THE COB +

Shuck corn just before cooking it. For easy clean-up, do this over a spread newspaper. Silk threads may be removed with a dampened paper towel.

Fill 4-quart pot about two-thirds full of water. Add <u>no</u> salt or sugar! Cover pan, set on burner on high heat.

When water boils, drop corn into pot. Do not cover. When water boils again, cook ears for 1 or 2 minutes (2 minutes for older corn). Remove pan from heat, cover. Let corn remain in water 5 to 10 minutes before serving. Serve with butter (lots) and paper napkins (lots).

+ COMMENTS +

1. If all corn is not eaten at once, extra ears can remain in water as long as 20 minutes and still be fine.

2. If you've cooked too much corn, save it for tomorrow. Hold ear steady in bowl in the sink. Cut off kernels as close to the cob as you can with a sharp knife. To serve, heat in butter in small skillet.

POST GRADUATE

IF YOU'RE BEGINNING to <u>like</u> to cook, and feel the elements of food are like parts of an orchestra now waiting, atremble, to vibrate to the lift of your own baton, here are some great performances for you.

Actually, this chapter contains a series of fine exercises, not whole symphonies. It will give you the ABC's of Roasting, the mathematics of Sauces, and a bird's-eye view of cooking in a wok. Also included are recipes for three dishes celebrated throughout the world: <u>veal parmigiana</u>, <u>coq au vin</u>, and <u>boeuf en daube</u> (pot roast). They have been re-interpreted to suit your tempo. As a final (trumpet) flourish, a few masterly techniques for leftovers.

Some of these recipes require extra equipment - a blender, a wok - and some unusual ingredients. Check the recipes thoroughly before beginning.

ROASTING EVERYTHING - ROASTING EVERYTHING - ROASTING EVERYTHING -

LAST NIGHT you had a preposterous dream: Your rich old Uncle Benny suddenly appeared in a mist. He was bearing a large, paper-wrapped load. Wordless, he deposited it on your kitchen counter, pointed to the oven, and vanished. You were weeping helplessly. You knew what terrors lurked within that gift's wrapping. It was a roast, and you were afraid of it. You awoke trembling, shaken. Right then you made a vow: "No roast will ever haunt me again. I will master it." And now you will.

As to proper roasting methods there are about as many divergent opinions as there are in politics. High-temperature roasting, or low-temperature roasting? To use a thermometer? To baste or not to baste? You could go crazy. But, vow in mind, you gotta start somewhere! Here are some basic rules plus a reliable roasting timetable. Follow these for now. In later years, develop your own refinements.

+ <u>BASIC RULES</u> +

1. Remove roast from refrigerator 1-2 hours before cooking, to let it warm to room temperature. It cooks faster that way.

2. Use a 13" × 9" × 2" pan. Use a <u>metal rack</u> inside your pan and place roast on it. (If roast sits on pan bottom it stews in its own fat and juices and becomes boiled and soggy.) If your pan is too small for your roast, borrow; a heavy roast squeezed into too small a pan is unmanageable.

3. Preheat oven to proper temperature for 10 minutes before you start roasting.

4. Make sure your oven registers properly. Many are faulty and are off by 25-50 degrees. Have it adjusted. (Phone your smiling gas or electric man.)

5. Season with salt and pepper <u>just</u> before you begin.

6. Basting <u>meat</u> is not necessary.

7. Basting <u>chicken</u> helps a lot!

8. Do <u>not</u> cover meat when roasting.

9. If using a meat thermometer, insert it in thickest part of roast. Do <u>not</u> let it touch a bone.

10. Roast meat fat side up, on <u>center</u> rack of oven.

11. Always let roast wait 10-15 minutes on counter before carving.

	+ TIMETABLE FOR ROASTING MEATS +		
	Oven Temperature (Fahrenheit)	Minutes per Pound	Thermometer Reading
BEEF			
rare	300	18 to 20	140 F.
medium		22 to 25	160
well-done		27 to 30	170
PORK, fresh	350	30 to 35	185
LAMB	300	30 to 35	180
	If you prefer pinker lamb, roast at 25 minutes per pound.		
VEAL	300	25 to 30	170

For a small roast, allow the longer period of cooking per pound.

For a large roast, allow the shorter period of cooking per pound.

+ <u>COMMENT</u> +

Remember the weight of your roast! Write it down.

+ <u>HINTS ON IMPROVING ROAST MEATS AND POULTRY</u> +

LAMB:

(Check timetable above. Use 13″ × 9″ × 2″ pan with metal rack.)

1. Leg of lamb can be stretched to many meals. Ask your meat man to cut off the shank end (for soup), and to cut some lamb chops (2-3) off the loin end. Roast the center section. Use leftovers to make lamb curry. (See <u>Heat-Wave Chicken Curry</u> in SUMMER SESSION, page 130.)

2. Before you roast lamb, peel and cut up 2 garlic cloves in thin slices (about 10-12). With a thinbladed knife, make a 1″ slit in lamb and insert garlic slice. Continue thus all over lamb. (If you make all the slits first, you'll forget where they are. So do one at a time.) Next, salt and pepper lamb on all sides. Set on rack, fat side up.

3. Peel some small potatoes. Roast them in pan bottom beside lamb <u>for the last hour of cooking</u>. Turn them over once to brown during cooking.

4. Or, serve lamb with warmed and drained can of white beans (cannellini).

5. Rolled leg or shoulder of lamb is prepared the same way as leg of lamb. Takes a little longer to cook. It's easier to carve.

6. For gravy see SAUCES! and GRAVY! page 136. Use beef broth.

BEEF:

(Check timetable, page 134. Use a 13″ × 9″ × 2″ pan with metal rack.)

1. Follow Basic Rules, page 133. Don't cover pan!

2. Roast potatoes with the roasting beef. Proceed as directed in suggestion # 3 for lamb.

3. Or, serve YORKSHIRE PUDDING with the beef. Shortcut: Buy small box popover mix. Whisk, in mixing bowl, with milk and egg according to package instructions. When beef is done, remove it to a platter. Discard metal rack. Pour popover mix into hot fat in roasting pan. Turn oven to 450. Bake on center rack for 10 minutes. Reduce heat to 350. Bake 15-20 minutes or until it puffs and is lightly brown. Cut in squares and serve with beef.

PORK:

(Check timetable, page 134. Use a 13″ × 9″ × 2″ pan with metal rack.)

1. Salt and pepper all over. Sprinkle with a favorite herb. Roast uncovered.

2. Pork and Gravy (page 137) are wonderful with Mashed Potatoes (page 71) and sauerkraut:

3. MARY JENNINGS' SAUERKRAUT: Buy a 1-lb. bag of sauerkraut. Simmer in its own juice 30 minutes. Cube 2 oz. rinsed salt pork and fry it till crisp over medium heat. Add salt pork to sauerkraut plus 1 peeled grated green apple, 1 peeled grated small potato, plus 1 peeled grated small onion. (Use large hole side of grater; or chop up all, fine.) Simmer 30 minutes, covered. Never boil!

VEAL

(Check timetable, page 134. Use a 13″ × 9″ × 2″ pan with metal rack.)

1. Salt and pepper veal. Dust all over with paprika (gives roast a nice browned effect). Crisscross 2 thick strips of bacon on top. (Bacon bastes veal, lends a nice flavor.)

2. Make gravy with Real Homemade Chicken Soup (page 28).

3. Veal is so nice with Buttered Noodles (page 57).

4. Have no bacon? Rub veal well with soft butter. Then salt, pepper, and paprika.

CHICKEN:

(You'll need the same 13″ × 9″ × 2″ pan with metal rack.)

1. Buy a 3½-lb. roasting chicken.

2. Remove giblets and neck (in sack inside chicken cavity). Salt and pepper well, inside and out. Cut off extra yellow fat and save. Use favorite herb (dried) inside and out.

3. A chicken roasts breast side up. Cut up yellow fat. Place strips on breast and across legs and thighs. Roast chicken on center rack of oven, uncovered, at 325 about 1 hour 15 minutes. (When you can wiggle a leg easily, chicken is done.)

4. Baste chicken twice (or more) with pan juices during roasting time.

5. For a really superb chicken leftover dish, try Jon's Chicken Casserole Supreme, page 147.

6. Chicken gravy, page 137.

TURKEY:

(Check pan size.)

1. If frozen, defrost overnight in refrigerator.

2. Remove inner sack with liver, giblets, and neck. Make soup with neck and giblets, page 28. Save liver and fry, cut in quarters, with onions for breakfast, or see page 85, Hugo's Chicken Livers Supreme.

3. Turkey doesn't need stuffing, but it's nice. Beginners: Use prepared package stuffings and follow directions.

4. Unless you live on a farm, your turkey will come with cooking instructions on wrapping. Follow them for cooking. Roast, uncovered, on center rack of oven, breast side up. Baste frequently.

5. Salt and pepper inside and out before stuffing. Remove extra yellow fat and place on breast and legs.

6. Make gravy, page 137. Use chicken broth.

7. A wonderful turkey leftover dish is on page 146: Andrea's Turkey Paella. Try it. Rewards!

DUCK:
(Use a 13″ × 9″ × 2″ pan with metal rack.)

1. Remove neck and inner sack. Make stock of innards (except liver), neck, a medium chopped onion, and 1 stalk chopped celery; simmer, covered, 2 hours with 2-3 cups water, plus 1 teaspoon salt. Use stock to make gravy. (Fry liver for breakfast.)

2. Remove excess duck fat and discard. Salt and pepper duck inside and out.

3. 2 medium peeled onions, quartered, plus 2 medium cored and quartered green apples, can be stuffed inside for added flavor.

4. Roast duck at 325 for 3½ hours, uncovered.

5. Don't baste! Pour off accumulated fat into a can. Heavy fat and grease clog drains and create large plumbing problems.

+ +

SAUCES! and GRAVY! - SAUCES! and GRAVY! - SAUCES! and GRAVY! - SAUCES! and

+ +

+ EVERYBODY'S FIRST SAUCE +

You might as well learn this now. It's what makes the world of sauces go round. The mechanics are also the basis for gravy.

It's a formula, folks: 2 to 2 to 1.

Hard, eh what?

While you're at it learn its proper name: Béchamel Sauce, also known as cream sauce and as medium white sauce. Here we go!

2 tablespoons butter	1 cup milk
2 tablespoons flour	Salt and pepper

Melt the butter over medium heat. Add flour. STIR 10 seconds. Slowly add milk, stirring constantly, till flour thickens (3-5 minutes). Voilà! Makes 1 cup; all formulas below make 1 cup.

+ COMMENTS +

1. If you want a thin sauce, change the formula to: 1 to 1 to 1.
2. If you want a thick sauce, change the formula to: 3 to 3 to 1.
3. If you want a cup of GRAVY:

2 tablespoons pan drippings (fat from pan in which meat cooked)
2 tablespoons flour

1 cup broth (made from stock), page 28, or from 1 teaspoon instant bouillon mix in 1 cup hot water

USING THE medium white (Béchamel) sauce formula, you can create any of the following:

+ MORNAY SAUCE +

Proceed as for Béchamel Sauce: When thickened add ½ cup grated cheese (Cheddar, American), ½ teaspoon Dijon mustard, ½ teaspoon Worcestershire sauce. Stir till cheese melts. (For fish, eggs, vegetables.)

+ VELOUTÉ SAUCE +

Proceed as for Béchamel Sauce, but substitute 1 cup fish stock (or 1 can clam juice) for the milk. Stir till thickened. No salt. (For fish.)

+ MUSTARD SAUCE +

Proceed as with Béchamel Sauce formula. Before you add milk, add ½ teaspoon dry mustard and ½ teaspoon Dijon mustard. STIR. Add milk. Cook, stirring, till thickened. (For fish.)

+ HERB SAUCE +

Proceed as for Béchamel Sauce. Before you add milk, add 1 teaspoon fresh herbs (parsley or dill, chopped), or ½ teaspoon dried herbs (tarragon, basil, or thyme). Stir with flour very briefly. Add milk. Stir till it thickens. (For vegetables, mostly, or chicken.)

+ TOMATO SAUCE +

Buy it! It's a pain to make. Hunt's is great.

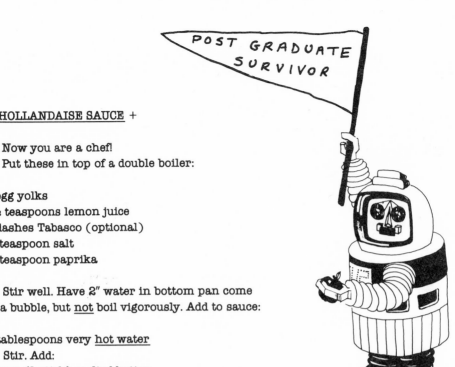

+ HOLLANDAISE SAUCE +

Now you are a chef!
Put these in top of a double boiler:

3 egg yolks
1½ teaspoons lemon juice
2 dashes Tabasco (optional)
¼ teaspoon salt
⅛ teaspoon paprika

Stir well. Have 2″ water in bottom pan come
to a bubble, but <u>not</u> boil vigorously. Add to sauce:

3 tablespoons very <u>hot water</u>
Stir. Add:
½ cup (1 stick) <u>melted</u> butter

You <u>must</u> stir to pan bottom <u>constantly</u> throughout cooking, 5-6 minutes. Don't let it cook too fast, or eggs will scramble. When thick (as melted fudge sauce), remove from heat. Put pan top in a bowl of cold water. Stir a minute more to cool down inner heat of eggs. Cover. Set on counter. Serve later at room temperature over hot vegetables. (Asparagus, broccoli, fish, anything!)

+ COMMENT +

A toasted English muffin + a thin slice of boiled ham + a poached egg + a topping of this sauce = <u>EGGS BENEDICT!</u>

+ MOUSSELINE SAUCE +

Princely! Make <u>Hollandaise Sauce</u>. Just before serving, whip ½ cup <u>whipping</u> (medium) <u>cream</u> till it's fluffy. Stir it gently into the Hollandaise. Salt only if necessary. (Fantastic on all vegetables. Try on cauliflower or broccoli. Also for fish.)

+ +
WOKING IT - WOKING IT - WOKING IT - WOKING IT - WOKING IT - WOKING IT -
+ +

MANY PEOPLE TODAY are using woks. A wok is not a funny noise, it is a kitchen utensil invented by the Chinese eons ago as a fuel-saving device. In the wok you can sauté, deep fry, steam, boil, even braise. Its bowl shape provides its versatility and assures its flash method of cooking. The heat is better contained, charging back and forth inside the bowl without dispersing, than in our Western pots.

The wok comes complete with a dome-shaped lid and a "ring collar" on which it sits to prevent tipping. The ring must have round holes in it to let air in under wok.

As compared to regular cooking, where preparation is short but cooking is long,

Chinese cooking is the reverse. Everything is chopped, minced, and sliced finely beforehand. At dinnertime, the production of the dish takes a maximum of 5 minutes. That's why you get fed so fast in a Chinese restaurant.

Once a Chinese gentleman was asked why he used chopsticks instead of a knife and fork. He said, "We prefer not to butcher at table."

If you buy a wok, be sure to get a decent booklet with it that explains the "seasoning" and care of the wok.

CHINESE INGREDIENTS:

Certain basic ingredients are essential to most recipes. They are garlic, fresh ginger, peanut or salad oil, salt, light soy sauce (Kikkoman is best), dry sherry, cornstarch, sugar, scallions, and broth (instant chicken bouillon). Without these you cannot proceed correctly. (Sesame oil is nice to have at hand. You do not cook it. It's a "perfume" and, like such, it evaporates with heat. You use a few drops after the dish is cooked.) Rice (Carolina long-grain) is a must!

There are many metal woks on the market. The best are made of iron, or cold-rolled carbon steel. The ideal size is 14" in diameter.

If you're out for speed and top nutrition, the wok is for you.

A constantly sharp knife and chopping block are essential.

If you go all-out for Chinese cooking, learn to use the Chinese cleaver; buy one of medium weight. And take some lessons on it first; find a friend who knows (you don't have to enroll in a school).

Here are two good "stir-fry" recipes to try with your wok. Wok on, wok on, with hope in your heart and you'll never wok alone. However, after all that, lacking a wok, you can do them right in your 12" skillet.

+ CHICKEN WITH VEGETABLES + (MOO GOO GAI PAN)

Serves 4. Delicate flavors mingle smoothly in this easy-to-prepare dish. (Cook 1½ cups rice before starting recipe; makes 3 cups.)

MAIN INGREDIENT:

1-lb. (1½ to 2 cups) sliced leftover chicken, OR 1 lb. raw chicken breasts

PREPARATION:

Slice leftover chicken into ¼" thick × 2" long rectangles.

OR: If using uncooked chicken, gently cut away skin and yellow fat. Discard. Bone chicken. (Using sharp knife, gently scrape-cut chicken from bone.) Cut chicken up into thin ¼" × 2" slices.

In small bowl, lightly beat 1 egg white. Add ¼ teaspoon salt, 1 teaspoon dry sherry wine, and 1 teaspoon cornstarch. Mix well together. Add chicken slices. Stir. Set aside.

Remove strings from ½ lb. snow peas. Wipe off and slice 12 mushrooms. Wash and thin-slice 2 stalks celery. Slice 12 water chestnuts (small can) into thin rounds. Peel and chop 1 clove garlic. Remove root ends and thin-slice 3 scallions.

Heat wok over high heat. Add salt. Add 2 tablespoons oil. Let it heat 30 seconds. Add snow peas, mushrooms, celery, and water chestnuts. Stir and fry, in a scooping motion with large spoon, 2 minutes. Remove vegetables from pan to plate.

Heat wok again. Add 2 tablespoons oil. Heat 30 seconds till bubbly. Add garlic, scallions, and chicken mixture. Stir-fry, scooping quickly for 1 minute. Chicken is done when white.

To wok add 2 teaspoons soy sauce plus ½ teaspoon sugar. Mix well with chicken.

Return vegetables to wok. Stir-fry quickly, mixing well, for 1 minute more. Remove to plate. Serve with rice.

+ + + + + + + + + + + +

+ CHINESE STEAK AND PEPPERS +

Serves 4. Harmonious flavors and contrasting textures. (Cook 1½ cups of rice before you start; makes 3 cups.)

INGREDIENTS and PROCEDURE:

Slice 1 lb. flank, round, or sirloin steak against the grain into pieces ⅛" thick and 2" long.

In mixing bowl: 1 tablespoon soy sauce, 1 teaspoon sugar, ½ teaspoon salt, 1 tablespoon cornstarch, 2 tablespoons dry sherry wine, 2 quarter-size slices peeled fresh ginger, chopped fine, 1 peeled chopped clove garlic, 1 tablespoon salad oil.

Mix together well. Add sliced meat and turn to coat meat thoroughly. Let sit and marinate 15 minutes.

Meanwhile: Remove seeds and stems of 2 green peppers. Slice ½" wide. Peel and slice 1 medium onion ½" wide. Slice ½ cup (2 oz.) water chestnuts into thin rounds. Set aside.

In a small bowl: Mix together 1 teaspoon salt, ¾ cup water, or chicken broth, 1 tablespoon cornstarch, 1 tablespoon soy sauce. Set aside.

Heat wok over high heat. Add 1 tablespoon oil. Tip wok by handles to slosh oil all around. Let oil heat 30 seconds. Add sliced peppers, onions, and water chestnuts. Stir and fry around in a scooping motion (2 minutes). Remove vegetables to a plate.

Reheat wok on high. Add 1 tablespoon oil for 30 seconds. Add beef mixture. Stir-fry about 3 minutes.

Stir liquid in the small bowl. Add to wok. Add precooked vegetables. Stir-fry 1 minute more, tossing all the time. Serve on rice.

+ +
BLENDING IT - BLENDING IT - BLENDING IT - BLENDING IT - BLENDING IT - BLEND
+ +

THE BLENDER IS ONE OF the most useful, time-saving kitchen aids ever invented. In it you can purée and liquefy practically anything. Most blenders come complete with instructions and recipes. Here are 4 recipes which make you a master chef in seconds.

+ EXCELLENT BLENDER MAYONNAISE + Takes 1-2 minutes

A culinary fact: That which you make yourself is far more economical than that which you buy. And, what's more, tastes better. So put your blender to work. Save $$ and enjoy!

INGREDIENTS:

1 large egg
½ teaspoon salt
¼ teaspoon pepper
⅛ teaspoon garlic powder (optional)

½ teaspoon imported mild mustard
(Dijon is best)
1½ cups salad oil (corn)
1 tablespoon lemon juice

PREPARATION:

Crack egg into blender container.
Add salt, pepper, garlic powder, and mustard. Cover.
Turn blender on high (5 seconds) to mix well. Uncover.
With blender on low: SLOWLY add oil in a thin stream. Pour carefully! When egg starts to grab the oil and the mixture thickens, you can pour a little faster. When oil is all in, add lemon juice, and blend 2 seconds more. (Stop when mixture is the consistency of mayonnaise.)
Refrigerate, covered. This will keep well for about one week.

+ + + + + + + + + + + +

+ BLUE CHEESE CREAMY SALAD DRESSING +   Takes 1-2 minutes

This makes the BEST tangy, creamy dressing in a matter of seconds. It's absolutely terrific on crisp washed spinach salad, or on your favorite salad greens.

INGREDIENTS:

2 scallions
1 cup salad oil
3 tablespoons lemon juice (or wine
    vinegar)

¼ teaspoon sugar (or omit)
1 teaspoon salt
3-oz. blue cheese (or Roquefort, the very
    top), crumbled

PREPARATION:

Remove root end of scallions and cut up, using the white and ¾ of the green part.
Put all ingredients into blender container in order given. Cover.
Turn on to high and run 1 minute, or till contents are well blended.
  Refrigerate, covered, till needed.

+ COMMENTS +

1. In making SPINACH SALAD, the addition of 2-3 raw sliced mushrooms per person, plus 1 strip fried, crumbled bacon per person, makes a super supper.
2. Garlic addicts often add 1 small, peeled, chopped clove of garlic to this dressing before blending. Garlic addicts are smart!

+ <u>SPEEDY PARTY PÂTÉ</u> +   Takes 10 minutes in all

Make this hours ahead. It needs time (2-4 hours) in the refrigerator to pull itself together and get elegant. Spread on plain, unsalted crackers like Carr's, and everyone will think it's the REAL, imported thing.

INGREDIENTS:

½ lb. liverwurst (Braunschweiger is best
    here)
3 scallions
¼ cup black pitted olives (buy the 8-oz.
    can)

2 tablespoons soft cream cheese
2 tablespoons sour cream
2 tablespoons brandy (A must! Borrow
    some.)

PREPARATION:

Cut up Braunschweiger liverwurst and put in blender container.

Remove root end of scallions. Cut up white and ¾ green part. Add to blender.

Drain olives. Put ¼ cup in blender. (Put remainder in small bowl in refrigerator and serve at party, as is. Nice nibbling.)

To blender add cream cheese, sour cream, and brandy. Cover.

Blend on <u>high</u> till everything is <u>pâté</u> smooth (1 minute).

Spoon into crock or bowl. Refrigerate 2-4 hours. If you have a sprig of parsley, pop it on top (for gourmet effect).

+ + + + + + + + + + + +

+ <u>PESTO SAUCE, WINTER STYLE</u> +

When fresh basil is unprocurable in the winter, this kissin' cousin to summer-style pesto is a very good thing indeed. It's an <u>uncooked</u> blender sauce which is mixed into the hot pasta. Try different pastas with it; for instance, the spiral shape called <u>fusilli</u>, or twists. One of Italy's GREAT sauces.

INGREDIENTS:

4-5 large cloves garlic
1 bunch parsley
1½ cups olive oil
2 tablespoons dried basil

2-oz. bottle pignoli (pine nuts) or small
    package fresh pignoli
4 oz. grated Parmesan cheese (plus some
    extra for pasta topping)
½ teaspoon salt

PREPARATION:

Peel and cut up garlic.
Rinse off parsley. Remove stems. Shake dry.
Add everything to blender in order given.
Run blender on <u>high</u> till sauce is smooth (1-2 minutes).
Refrigerate, covered, till needed. This makes enough sauce for 2 lbs. of cooked pasta,
or 8 servings.

+ <u>COMMENTS</u> +

1. You'll need <u>extra</u> grated Parmesan. After you've cooked the pasta and mixed in the
pesto sauce, dust everything with it, on top.
2. Leftover sauce freezes well. Use to flavor soups, or on broiled meat and fish, or as
a spread on toasted French bread.

+ +
INTERNATIONAL TRIO - Classics - INTERNATIONAL TRIO - Classics - INTERNATIONAL
+ +

+ <u>VEAL PARMIGIANA ZIPPO</u> +   Preparation: 15 minutes
                                               Cooking: 15 minutes

<u>Serves 2-4</u>. You hit the ground running with this zipped-up version of a world-famous
dish. A great facsimile of the original recipe. Now <u>you</u> can do it too.

INGREDIENTS:

4 tablespoons butter or margarine   16-oz. jar Ragú's spaghetti sauce
4 breaded veal cutlets (see frozen section 4 slices mozzarella cheese
    of market's meat department)

PREPARATION:

In large (12″) ovenproof skillet, melt butter over medium-high heat.
Add defrosted veal to skillet. Turn down heat to medium. Sauté on each side (about 5
minutes) till veal is light brown.
Warm sauce in a small saucepan, 1-2 minutes. Pour sauce over veal.
Set a slice of cheese on each piece of veal.
Put skillet in oven on rack about 7″ from top heating element. Turn oven to broil.
When the cheese is melted (keep watching here; it happens <u>fast!</u>), remove and serve.
Hope you've made a <u>green salad</u> and have some crusty <u>Italian bread</u> on hand.

+ + + + + + + + + + + +

+ <u>CHICKEN BAKED IN WINE</u> +　　　　Preparation: 15 minutes
(COQ AU VIN)　　　　　　　　　　Cooking: 55 minutes

<u>Serves 4</u>. The French name is <u>coq au vin</u>. You see it on so many menus. You've tried it and really enjoyed it. But you think it must be hard to do. It isn't; not with this easily assembled recipe. Now, you're a French chef!

INGREDIENTS:

2½- to 3-lb. chicken fryer, cut up
3 tablespoons butter or margarine
10 small white onions or 8-oz. can,
　　drained.
1 large clove garlic
10½-oz. can chicken broth (College Inn)
4-oz. can mushrooms

⅓ cup dry red wine (like Burgundy)
1 bay leaf
¼ teaspoon thyme
½ teaspoon salt
½ cup water
¼ cup flour

PREPARATION:

Turn oven to 350.

Rinse chicken under cold-water tap. Pat <u>very</u> dry with paper towels. Cut off extra fat.

In large, ovenproof skillet, melt butter over medium-high heat. Add chicken pieces, skin side down. Sauté in butter till browned, about 5 minutes. (Check now and then and adjust heat.)

Turn chicken. Brown on other side.

Peel onions and garlic. Mince garlic into small bits.

To skillet add chicken broth, mushrooms (drained), wine, whole onions, chopped garlic, bay leaf, thyme, and salt.

Cover. Bake on center rack of oven at 350 for 35 minutes.

Meanwhile, in a cup mix flour and water thoroughly.

Remove skillet from oven. Add flour-water mixture. If using <u>canned</u> onions, add here. Stir well.

At stove, over medium-high heat, cook chicken, uncovered, till sauce thickens. (Watch it! Don't let it burn.) This takes about 4-5 minutes.

Remove bay leaf and serve.

+ <u>COMMENTS</u> +

1. All you need with this: <u>small boiled potatoes</u> and a crisp <u>green salad</u> with <u>Garlic Dressing</u> (page 31).

2. For a vegetable side dish, the French would surely serve the <u>Carrot-Turnip Combo</u> on page 65.

3. If you don't know what to do with the rest of the wine (!), give it to your landlady, corked.

+ <u>POT ROAST PERFECTION</u> +   Preparation: 20 minutes
  (BOEUF EN DAUBE)   Cooking: 3 hours

<u>Serves 4-6</u>. There is nothing more satisfying on a cold winter night, or after a long day of studying, than a meal all ready for you. Pot roast is the answer. It simmers independently for 2½ hours and greets you with a smile of mingled flavors that make you feel ravenously hungry. Prepare ahead.

INGREDIENTS:

2 tablespoons butter
2 tablespoons oil (corn)
2 large onions
2 large cloves garlic
2½- to 3-lb. piece of chuck, boneless
2 large carrots
2-3 stalks celery and leaves

1 small can (4 oz.) tomato juice (or ½ cup dry red wine)
½ teaspoon each salt and pepper
½ teaspoon basil
1 bay leaf
3 medium potatoes (tennis-ball size)

PREPARATION:

In a <u>heavy</u> 12″ skillet, melt butter with oil over medium-high heat.

Peel and chop up onions and garlic. Put them in skillet. Cook over medium heat till onions are wilted but not browned.

Remove onions with slotted spoon. Save for later.

Put meat in skillet. Turn heat up to medium high. Brown on both sides (5 minutes each). Lift with cooking fork to check, now and then.

While meat browns: Scrape carrots. Cut up small (1″ pieces).

Wash and dry celery. Slice, with leaves, into 1″ pieces.

Remove meat to a plate.

Return cooked onions and garlic to skillet, add raw carrots and celery. Place browned meat on top of vegetables.

Pour tomato juice (or wine) over all. Add salt, pepper, basil, and bay leaf.

Turn <u>up</u> heat. Bring to a bubble. Quickly turn <u>down</u> heat. Cover. Simmer on <u>low</u> heat 2½ hours.

Thirty minutes before dinner, peel and cut up potatoes in bite-size pieces. Add to meat. Push potatoes down into accumulated liquid. Cover. Simmer 30 minutes more.

Remove bay leaf. Serve when you're ready. It can wait.

Need more salt? Add some, judiciously.

+ <u>COMMENT</u> +

Pot roast is famous for enjoying being ignored. Therefore you'll find it is even better reheated the following day. Or eat it cold, in a sandwich.

+ + + + + + + + + + +

THESE ARE ACTUALLY completely possible for <u>undergraduate</u> survivors. They link up with the recipes in this chapter, as you will see, and they serve a small crowd (4-6), so they qualify for a party menu. <u>Yes</u>, leftovers are suitable ingredients for guests.

+ <u>MARTHA CLARK'S TOFU QUICHE</u> +   Preparation: 15 minutes
                                              Baking: 25 minutes

<u>Serves 4-6</u>. Tofu is meat's equivalent. Adding it to a vegetable dish gives you instant protein, a fact the Japanese and Chinese have known forever. Although tasteless in itself, it combines with other foods for wonderful results in texture and nutrition. Here's a perfect example.

INGREDIENTS:

1 lb. tofu   1 cup milk
8 oz. Monterey Jack cheese, shredded   ½ teaspoon salt
½ cup bread crumbs   ¼ teaspoon pepper
4 scallions, chopped fine (use whites and
        green parts)

PREPARATION:

Turn oven to 350.
Grease a 9″ square cake pan, or round pie pan.
In mixing bowl, mash tofu well with a dinner fork.
Add shredded cheese, bread crumbs, chopped scallions, milk, salt, and pepper. Stir to mix thoroughly.
Pour into cake pan. Bake on center rack in 350 oven for 25 minutes, uncovered. Remove.
Let stand on counter 10-15 minutes to get firm before cutting.

+ <u>COMMENT</u> +

This can be made early in the day and reheated at dinner time in a 325 oven for 15 minutes.

+ + + + + + + + + + + +

+ <u>ANDREA'S TURKEY PAELLA</u> +   Preparation: 20 minutes
                                          Cooking: 10 minutes

<u>Serves 4</u>. If you order paella in a Madrid restaurant, you can get severe malnutrition waiting for it to appear. Always a mixture of seafood and chicken, plus . . . the recipe must begin: "First dive into the sea and catch . . ." You'll like this 30-minute cut-down version.

LINE UP YOUR INGREDIENTS:

2 cups leftover turkey (or chicken)
½ lb. pepperoni (or 1 stick)
1 medium onion
1 large green pepper
3 stalks celery
3 cloves garlic

2 tablespoons butter, margarine, or oil
1 teaspoon dried basil
1 small can (4 oz.) sliced olives
6½-oz. can chopped clams
1 package Near East Rice Pilaf Mix or
    Spanish Rice Pilaf Mix

PREPARATION:

Cook pilaf mix according to package directions.

Meanwhile: Cut up turkey into bite-size chunks. Slice pepperoni, thin.

Peel and chop onion. Seed and stem green pepper and chop up. Slice celery, and leaves too. Peel and chop up garlic.

In large saucepan, melt butter over medium-high heat. Add pepperoni, onion, green pepper, celery, garlic, and basil. Cook, stirring now and then, for 5 minutes.

Add turkey, sliced olives, clams AND juice, and cook together 1 minute more, stirring.

Turn the rice pilaf into the pot. Mix together well.

Remove from heat. Cover. Serve steaming. (You will eat it all!)

+ + + + + + + + + + +

+ JON'S CHICKEN CASSEROLE SUPREME +   Preparation: 5 minutes
                                        Baking: 30 minutes

Serves 4. From Boston College, this is an ideal leftovers recipe. It assembles almost instantly and develops a superb new flavor in the baking. It is equally good done with turkey, veal, or ham leftovers.

INGREDIENTS:

2 cups cooked chicken (about half a
    chicken)
¾ cup mayonnaise
¼ cup water
1 can cream of mushroom soup

4-oz. can sliced mushrooms, optional
1 tablespoon Worcestershire sauce
¼ teaspoon Tabasco
½ teaspoon salt
8-oz. package medium-broad egg noodles
2-3 tablespoons grated Parmesan cheese

PREPARATION:

Grease a 2-quart casserole. Turn oven on to 350.

Dice up cooked chicken. Put it into casserole.

Add: mayonnaise, water, mushroom soup, sliced mushrooms, and juice from can, Worcestershire sauce, Tabasco, and salt. Stir to mix ingredients well.

Boil noodles according to package directions (8 minutes). Drain into sieve at sink. Add noodles to casserole. Mix all together.

Dust top of noodles with Parmesan cheese.

Cover casserole. Bake on center rack of oven at 350 for 30 minutes. Remove and serve.

BACK IN THE DARK AGES (1973), <u>The Campus Survival Cookbook #1</u> was published and we got fan mail! We really did, and from people of all ages, not only students. We were so pleased to learn that the book was serving its purpose, encouraging people to cook and cope and SURVIVE and enjoy it. Here present, the seven recipes from that book which got the biggest raves.

+ DON'T-CLAM-UP SPAGHETTI +

Preparation: 10 minutes
Cooking: 10 minutes

Serves 2. A classic Mediterranean meal. The first forkful of clam spaghetti doesn't send you anywhere because it takes a few bites for the subtle flavors to accumulate. Then, ecstasy! Make the garlic bread and salad first, so you can sit right down the minute the sauce is ready. That takes about 10 minutes.

LINE UP YOUR INGREDIENTS:

½ lb. thin spaghetti
3 medium garlic cloves
¼ cup chopped fresh parsley
2 cans minced clams (7 oz. each)

3 tablespoons butter
3 tablespoons oil
3 oz. (½ cup) grated Italian cheese
    (Romano or Parmesan)

PREPARATION:

Boil 8 cups of water. Add spaghetti. Boil 8 minutes, uncovered. Drain spaghetti at sink. Run under hot water. Leave in sieve.

Meanwhile: Chop up garlic cloves. Chop fresh parsley. Open cans of minced clams. Drain. SAVE JUICE!

In large skillet, melt butter over medium heat. Add oil. Add garlic and cook 1-2 minutes. Watch it. Don't let it burn.

Add parsley. Stir quickly. Add clam juice. Turn heat down to low and simmer, covered, for 5 minutes.

Add clams. Cook 1 minute more. Remove from heat.

Add cooked spaghetti. Stir well. Salt to taste. Serve at once. Top with grated cheese at table.

+ + + + + + + + + + +

+ GOURMET PORK CHOPS GEHRECKE +

Preparation: 5 minutes
Cooking: 45 minutes

Serves 2-4. Frank Gehrecke, at Northwestern, handed us this winner. Here are plain old pork chops gussied up and tasting like $9.00 a plate. Their Grand Marnier (that's a liqueur) flavor is created by the addition of orange juice.

LINE UP YOUR INGREDIENTS:

4 pork chops (center cut), ½" thick
1 teaspoon salt
½ teaspoon pepper

½ cup flour
3 tablespoons butter
2 cups orange juice

PREPARATION:

Scrape both sides of chops lightly with knife to remove tiny bone particles. Cut off excess fat, leaving a ⅛" rim.

In paper bag mix: salt, pepper, and flour. Shake each chop in bag till coated with mixture.

Melt butter in large (12") skillet over medium heat. Brown chops in skillet, 5 minutes each side.

Add 1½ cups of the orange juice. Bring to a boil on high heat. Turn heat down to low. Simmer chops <u>un</u>covered for 45 minutes.

+ <u>COMMENTS</u> +

1. If too much orange juice evaporates while cooking, add ½ cup more. You should expect to end up with ½ to ¾ cup of orange sauce in the skillet from the juice.

2. You are advised here to buy center-cut pork chops because, though not the cheapest, they're the best buy, having the least fat and bone.

+ + + + + + + + + + + +

+ <u>TAMALE PIE SAN DIEGO U.</u> +   Preparation: 15 minutes
                                        Cooking: 1 hour
                                        Waiting: 45 minutes

<u>Serves 6-8</u>. This casserole-type recipe can be made and served in a skillet or roasting pan. A firm, thick pudding, it is redolent with mouth-watering flavors of corn, cheese, and Mexican seasonings. Although it has a special affinity with ham, it can be equally successful served with chicken or turkey. Please note its "waiting time" above. This is absolutely necessary in the firming up process. Otherwise, you have soup!

LINE UP YOUR INGREDIENTS:

2 cans or jars tamales (13-oz. size)   1 small can tomato sauce (8 oz.)
2 medium cans <u>creamed</u> corn (1 lb.)   1 cup yellow corn meal
1 medium can pitted black olives   ½ lb. Cheddar cheese
4 tablespoons butter (½ stick)

PREPARATION:

Preheat oven to 350.

Open all cans and jars. Drain off olive juice. Cut olives in half. Grate cheese on grater's largest holes, or chop in small pieces.

Using 9" × 13" roasting pan or largest (12") iron skillet, melt butter over medium heat at stove. Remove pan to counter. Add cheese, corn, halved olives, tomato sauce, cornmeal.

Wash hands. Now dump in tamales and all juices. Remove husks (or wrappings). With fingers, break tamales into small pieces. Stir all together till well mixed. Place pie on middle oven rack, uncovered, for 1 hour.

Remove to fireproof surface. Pie will be a bit runny; allow to cool (and harden) 45 minutes or more. Fifteen minutes before serving, return to 350 oven to warm through.

+ + + + + + + + + + +

+ <u>VERY-LITTLE-COIN MASTERPIECE</u> +   Preparation: 30 minutes
                                          Cooking: 40 minutes

<u>Serves 6</u>. This is the kind of dish that might be served to you in Switzerland or Aspen at an après-ski party. It's hot sausage and sliced potatoes surrounded with a bubbling melted cheese sauce - inexpensive yet superb. <u>Note</u>: You will need a 9″ × 13″ × 2″ baking dish. Measure your roasting pan. It should substitute nicely.

INGREDIENTS:

2 large onions
4 tablespoons (½ stick) butter or
    margarine
1½ lb. kielbasa sausage (or Italian garlic
    type)
Three 1-lb. cans sliced white potatoes

4 eggs
2 cups (1 pint) light cream
½ teaspoon salt
¼ teaspoon pepper
2 oz. (½ cup) grated Swiss cheese

PREPARATION:

Do this <u>2 hours</u> before dinner: Peel and slice onions. Melt butter in skillet on medium heat. Add onions. Cook gently 4-5 minutes till onions are just tender but not browned. Stir a bit.

Slice sausage thickly (about 1″). Grease baking dish or roasting pan. Open and drain cans of potatoes.

Arrange cooked onions, sliced sausage, and potatoes in concentric circles in baking dish.

In mixing bowl, beat together eggs, cream, salt and pepper till well mixed. Pour into baking dish, covering all ingredients with mixture.

Grate Swiss cheese. Sprinkle it on top. <u>Refrigerate 1 hour</u>.

Heat oven to 375. Bake the "Masterpiece" for 40 minutes.

+ + + + + + + + + + +

+ <u>JON'S CHICKEN SPARERIBS</u> +   Preparation: 5 minutes
                                     Marinating: 15 minutes (or all day)
                                     Cooking: 45 minutes

<u>Serves 2</u>. This cheap and easy chicken dish comes out brown and succulent. Eat it with

your fingers, go Oriental with a side bowl of rice. Note that you can cook at once; or prepare in the A.M. and let wings sit in the marinade all day.

LINE UP YOUR INGREDIENTS:

1½ to 2 lb. chicken wings
¼ cup soy sauce

½ cup Boone's Farm Apple Wine, or honey
Some butter

PREPARATION:

Under cold tap water, wash chicken wings. Dry well.

In mixing bowl, measure the soy sauce, apple wine or honey. Stir well.

Add chicken wings to this marinade, and let sit at room temperature at least 15 minutes, but the longer the better.

Preheat oven to 400. Grease large (12″) skillet with a bit of butter.

Place chicken wings flat, not overlapping, in skillet. Spoon 2-3 tablespoons of marinade over chicken.

Place in oven. Bake 15 minutes. Baste wings with 2-3 more tablespoons of marinade, and bake 15 minutes more. Repeat basting process again, bake another 15 minutes (45 minutes in all).

Serve with, or on top of . . .

+ RICE +

Bring to boil 1 cup Uncle Ben's converted rice in 2 cups water. Turn to low heat, and simmer, covered, 20 minutes.

Add 1 tablespoon butter. Stir and serve, or keep warm, by covering, till wings are done.

+ + + + + + + + + + + +

+ SPAGHETTI MYSTERIOSO +   Preparation: 10 minutes
                                  Cooking: 50 minutes

Serves 4-6. This tastes like a fine spaghetti with meat sauce and was invented by mountain folk of Sicily who seldom eat meat because they're flat broke. (Don't tell anyone it contains eggplant and no one will ever guess.)

LINE UP YOUR INGREDIENTS:

2 garlic cloves
1 lb. eggplant
½ cup cooking oil
Two (1-lb.) cans tomatoes
2 green peppers

3 teaspoons oregano (heaping)
1 teaspoon salt (heaping)
½ teaspoon pepper (heaping)
1 lb. spaghetti (thin, e.g. spaghettini)

SAUCE:

The sauce can be put together in 10 minutes if you've learned how to chop round objects (page 16): Peel and dice garlic cloves. Peel and dice eggplant (as you would an onion). Open tomato cans.

In large (12″) skillet, heat oil over medium heat. Cook garlic pieces 1 minute or until just golden.

Add diced eggplant, then tomatoes and their juice. Stir well, breaking up tomatoes. While this cooks, wash green peppers, cut in half, remove seeds. Slice and dice peppers, stir them in at once.

Let mixture come to a good boil, over high heat, then turn down to medium heat. Cover pan, simmer, stirring occasionally, 30 to 40 minutes or until eggplant is soft and mushy.

Add seasonings - oregano, salt, and pepper.

Stir well and cook 10 more minutes. Serve over spaghetti.

SPAGHETTI:

Fifteen minutes before sauce is ready, get 6 to 8 cups salted water boiling in large saucepan. Add spaghetti. Stir to separate. Cook until just tender, 8 minutes (taste it).

To serve: Drain spaghetti. Pour half the sauce into a large casserole or the roasting pan. Add spaghetti and rest of sauce. Clean skillet with ¼ cup water, add to sauce. Mix very well with a couple of spoons. Serve.

+ COMMENTS +

1. Reheat in small quantities in a saucepan, or in oven, stirring in a teaspoon of water if it seems dry.

2. This is one spaghetti which doesn't seem to call for grated cheese, but chunks of a hard-crust bread are a nice addition.

3. To prepare this the authentic Sicilian way: Use just ½ teaspoon salt in sauce. For last 10 minutes of cooking, add 3 anchovy fillets, minced; 1 tablespoon capers; ½ cup sliced Italian black olives. But the recipe doesn't have to have all these rarities to make it good.

The way to chop an onion is FAST (page 16).

++++++++++++++++++++++++++++++

+ GRANNY'S CREAMY DREAMY CHEESECAKE PIE +

Preparation: 15 minutes
Baking: 30 minutes
Refrigerate: several hours

Serves 8 or 16. This creamy, cold delight should be made several hours ahead or the day before to ensure that it is icy cold. A cheesecake is usually served in slim wedges because it is so rich, therefore this quantity will serve 16 people. To serve 8, make it in two 8" pie pans, freeze one for later use. (See Comment 1.)

INGREDIENTS FOR CRUST:

⅓ box graham crackers, or use 2 cups precrushed graham-cracker crumbs

¼ lb. (1 stick) butter (or margarine)

Grease a 10" (or two 8") pie pans thoroughly inside with a piece of butter or margarine.

On flat clean surface: Use either rolling pin, bottle, or fists and fingers to pound graham crackers till they're crushed fine. Measure 2 cups.

Melt stick of butter in skillet over medium heat. Remove from heat. Add graham-cracker crumbs. Stir to mix well.

Line the greased pie pan with crumb mixture on bottom and sides. With back of spoon, press firmly to get it even all over.

INGREDIENTS FOR FILLING:

2 eggs
1 large and 1 small package cream
    cheese (at room temperature)

1 pint (2 cups) sour cream
¾ cups sugar
2 teaspoons vanilla extract

PREPARATION:

Preheat oven to 350.

In large mixing bowl, beat eggs till foamy. (Wire whisk does a good job.)

Add packs of soft cream cheese. Mash with fork till gloppy. Then stir and mash till eggs are incorporated into cream cheese.

Add sour cream, sugar, and vanilla. Beat till soft and mixed, with very few lumps. Pour filling into crust of crumb mixture.

Bake on center rack of oven, at 350. Done in 30 minutes. Remove from oven. Let cool on counter for ½ hour. Refrigerate.

+ COMMENTS +

1. To freeze soft-top cakes and pies without marring surface, freeze unwrapped. When rigid, wrap completely in foil.

2. To be extra fancy, top cheesecake with a couple of tablespoons of (thawed) frozen strawberries.

+ + + + + + + + + + +

BASTE: Spoon small quantities of liquid over food.

BOILING: When large bubbles appear on heated liquids. (Slow boiling is as effective and more economical than rapid boiling, since less heat is lost through escape of watery vapor.)

BRAISE: Cook, tightly covered, in small quantity of liquid (in oven, or over direct heat).

BROIL: Cook over a fire, or in the stove under direct(broiler) heat. PANBROIL: Cook in a pan on stove top, with only enough fat to keep food from sticking.

DEEP FRY: Cook food immersed in enough very hot oil to cover food.

FRY: Cook food in skillet with small amount of hot butter or oil. (See SAUTÉ.)

GREASE CASSEROLE: Pour a teaspoon or so of cooking oil on plastic wrap or paper towel. Rub this all over interior of casserole or pan.

MARINATE: Soak food in a liquid that adds flavor.

PARBOIL: Cook food partially either in boiling water or in its own juices (oysters, scallops, etc.) for a very short time.

DEGLAZE: Add a small amount of liquid to pan in which you have been cooking something. Turn heat to high, and stir to loosen and incorporate the taste-rich bits left on pan bottom.

ROAST: Cook in an oven; food is uncovered. See Timetable for Roasting Meats page 134.

SAUTÉ: Like "fry." Cook in a small quantity of fat in a pan over direct heat. Sauté comes from the French word sauter "to jump." French cooks shake the pan constantly to prevent too much absorption of fat.

SEAR: Subject surface to intense heat. One first "sears" meat to seal in juices and brown the surface in both sautéing and roasting.

SIMMER: Cook on stove top just below the boiling point; few bubbles should appear.

STEAM: Cook over boiling water. You can steam in a double boiler or in a steamer basket.

STEW: Cook, covered, in more liquid than "braising," at a low temperature, for several hours. One stews tougher meats and poultry to tenderize them.

Andrea's turkey paella, 146-147
Avocados, guacamole, 88-89

Bean(s):
    salad, 126
    -sausage chowder, Lucile's, 110
Beef:
    boeuf en daube, 145
    bunless burgers, 32-33
    Chinese steak and peppers, 140
    chipped, on toast, 86-87
    frozen burger loaf, 17
    Middle East meatballs, 46-47
    pastitsio, 95-96
    peasant meat loaf, 64-65
    pot roast perfection, 145
    roast
        how to improve, 135
        timetable for, 134
    survival #2 casserole, 59-60
Boeuf en daube, 145
Bread, 104-105
    fast survival, 104-105
    flash beer, 104
    French
        hot, 73
        pizzas, 114
    garlic, 31-32
    Italian
        herbed, 39
        hot, 35
    Stephanie's perfect banana, 105
    toasted pita, 69
Broccoli:
    buttered chopped, 61
    Chinese, 44-45
    chowder Andy, 69
Brunch menus, 84-87

Brussels sprouts, 54

Cabbage, southern-style, 76
Cakes:
    anonymous, 80
    granny's creamy dreamy cheesecake
        pie, 154
    old-fashioned icebox, 79-80
    peach shortcake express, 81
Carrot-turnip combo, 65
Cheese:
    blue, creamy salad dressing, 141
    macaroni and, primavera, 61
    omelet with, 24
    soufflé, fake, 43-44
Chicken:
    baked in wine, 144
    coq au vin, 144
    heat-wave curry, 130-131
    herb-baked, 27
    Hugo, braised Italian, 41-42
    Jon's casserole supreme, 147
    Marie's paprika, in yogurt sauce, 67
    moo goo gai pan, 139-140
    roast, hints on improving, 135
    salad, 123
    schizo, 99
    6-minute cold-cooked, 121-122
    tarragon sauté, 56-57
    thawing, 18
    with vegetables, 139-140
Chicken livers, Hugo's supreme, 85
Chicken wings, Jon's spareribs, 151-152
Chili-in-a-pocket, 113
Clams, don't-clam-up spaghetti, 149
Collard greens, 37-38
Cooking terms, 155
Coq au vin, 144

Corn:
    on the cob, 132
    niblets, 63
    fritters, 76

Desserts, 77-83
    anonymous (a cake), 80
    apple crisp, 77-79
    blueberry cobbler, 83
    Florian Applegate's hot fudge sauce,
        82-83
    granny's creamy dreamy cheesecake
        pie, 154
    grapes in brown sugar cream, 80-81
    hasty mocha icing, 82
    McCrystle's midnight shotgun special,
        77
    old-fashioned icebox cake, 79-80
    peach shortcake express, 81
Duck, roast, hints on improving, 136

Eggplant:
    Marie's casserole, 72-73
    oven-fried slices, 68
    spaghetti mysterioso, 152-153
Eggs:
    baked, 23
    Benedict, 138
    cowboy, 84-85
    fried, 23
    hard-boiled, 24
    -mayonnaise dressing, 101
    omelet with cheese, 24
    peasant omelet, 86
    poached, 23-24
    Serbian presnack, 94
    soft-boiled, 23
    whole world salad, 122-123
Enchiladas, Jenny's, 89-92

Fettucini, 49
Fish:
    easy Parmesan, 36
    frozen, defrosting, 36
    dilled, in foil, 74
    Ruthie's Louisiana Creole, 62
    sea food chowder, 107-108
    See also names of fish
Florian Applegate's hot fudge sauce, 82-83
Freezing food, 17-18

French bread:
    hot, 73
    pizzas, 114

Granny's creamy dreamy cheesecake pie, 154
Gravy:
    cream, 27
    sour-cream, 53
Green peas, buttered, 28-29
Guacamole, 88-89

Ham:
    butt, baked cottage, 75-76
    chunky-style salad, 123
    no-problem glazed baked, 102
Hugo's chicken livers supreme, 85

Italian bread:
    herbed, 39
    hot, 35

Jenny's enchiladas, 89-92
Jenny's Mexican rice, 91
Jon's chicken casserole supreme, 147
Jon's chicken spareribs, 151-152

Kasha, 53-54
Kitchen equipment, selecting, 9-15
Kitchen measurements, how to figure, 160

Lamb, roast:
    hints on improving, 134
    timetable for, 134
Lasagna, miracle skillet, 38-39
Lentils, 73
Lettuce, iceberg, with Russian dressing, 65
Lucile's sausage-bean chowder, 110

Macaroni:
    and cheese primavera, 61
    salad, 129
McCrystle's midnight shotgun special, 77
Marie's chicken paprika in yogurt sauce,
    67
Marie's eggplant casserole, 72-73
Marion's pork chop dream, 100-101
Martha Clark's tofu quiche, 146
Mary Jennings' sauerkraut, 135
Mayonnaise:
    -egg dressing, 101
    excellent blender, 140-141

Meat loaf, peasant, 64-65
Meats:
    freezing, 18
    roast
        hints on improving, 134-136
        timetable for, 134
    selecting, 19-20
Mip's summer bounty bouquet, 129-130
Moo goo gai pan, 139-140

Paella, Andrea's turkey, 146-147
Party foods, 88-103
Pâté, speedy party, 142
Pesto sauce, winter-style, 142-143
Pilaf:
    bulgur wheat, 47-48
    rice, 63
Pizza:
    French bread, 114
    one-handed, 114
Pork:
    roast
        hints on improving, 135
        timetable for, 134
    Russian roast, with sour-cream gravy,
        53
Pork chops:
    gourmet Gehrecke, 149-150
    Marion's dream, 100-101
Pork ribs, barbecued, 70-71
Potato(es):
    baked, 33
    boiled, 28
    chunky brown, 51-52
    diced creamed, 37
    home-fried, 74-75
    mashed, 71
    salad, 128-129

Quiche:
    crustless
        easy-ola, 30
        square, 87
    Martha Clark's tofu, 146
    spinach pie, 58

Rice:
    brown, 67-68
    carefree oven, 100
    fluffy white, 42

Jenny's Mexican, 91
    pilaf, 63
Roast meats, hints on improving, 134-136
Ruthie's Louisiana fish Creole, 62

Salad dressing:
    blue cheese creamy, 141
    egg-mayonnaise, 101
    excellent blender, 140-141
    French, traditional, 31
    herb, 98
    Italian, 48, 49-50
        creamy, 127
    plain, 35
    Russian, 65
    Thousand Island, 127-128
Salads:
    bean sprout, 45-46
    chef, 126-127
    chicken, 123
    chick-pea, 58-59
    chunky-style ham, 123
    creamy coleslaw, 71-72
    "George," 95
    iceberg lettuce with Russian dressing,
        65
    macaroni, 129
    mixed greens, 101
    for pita bread, 116-117
    potato, 128-129
    salmon cum laude, 123-124
    spinach, 35, 141
        A+, 96-97
    string beans with Italian dressing, 48
    3-bean, 126
    tomato-watercress, 49-50
    tossed greens with diced tomatoes,
        30-31
    tri-colored, 52
    tuna
        original Bernadette, 124-125
        vegetable and, 125
    turkey, 123
    whole world egg, 122-123
Salmon:
    loaf, 50
    salad cum laude, 123-124
Sandwiches:
    good guy's western, 115-116
    hot torpedo, 116
    Kongwich, 115

Sauces:
    Béchamel, 136-137
    cold, for spaghetti, 131
    cream, 136-137
      with crunch, 51
    everybody's first, 136-137
    Florian Applegate's hot fudge, 82-83
    herb, 137
    Hollandaise, 138
    medium white, 136-137
    Mornay, 137
    Mousseline, 138
    mustard, 137
    pesto, winter-style, 142-143
    tomato, 137
    velouté, 137
    yogurt, 46-47, 67
Sauerkraut, Mary Jennings', 135
Sausages:
    -bean chowder, Lucile's, 110
Sea food chowder, 107-108
Serbian presnack, 94
Soufflé:
    fake cheese, 43-44
    grits, 103
Soups, 106-112
    broccoli chowder Andy, 69
    fideos, 108-109
    gazpacho, 119
      instant, 25
    icy cream of cucumber, 119-120
    juanaveetch, 121
    lentil pep-up, 107
    Lucile's sausage-bean chowder, 110
    minestrone magnifico, 110-111
    old-fashioned split pea, 106-107
    sea food chowder, 107-108
    survival bone, 112
    vichyssoise, 118-119
Sour-cream gravy, 53
Spaghetti:
    bacon, Chris and Andrea, 97-98
    with cold sauce, 131
    don't-clam-up, 149
    marinara, 34-35

    mysterioso, 152-153
Spinach:
    fresh buttered, 42-43
    pie, 58
    salad, 35, 141
      A+, 96-97
Split peas, old-fashioned soup, 106-107
Stephanie's perfect banana bread, 105
String beans:
    in herb butter, 33-34
    salad with Italian dressing, 48
Summer foods, 118-132

Tabouleh, 117
Tamale pie San Diego U., 150-151
Toast, milk, 25
Tofu, Martha Clarke's quiche, 146
Tomato sauce, 137
Tuna salad:
    original Bernadette, 124-125
    vegetable and, 125
Turkey:
    Andrea's paella, 146-147
    roast, hints on improving, 135-136
    salad, 123
Turnip-carrot combo, 65

Veal:
    Parmigiana zippo, 143
    roast
      hints on improving, 135
      timetable for, 134
Vegetables:
    chicken with, 139-140
    Mip's summer bounty bouquet, 129-130
    and tuna salad, 125
    See also names of vegetables

Woks, 138-140

Yogurt sauce, 46-47, 67
Yogurt cheese, 25
Yorkshire pudding, 135

Zucchini, southern-style, 57

t. = teaspoon
T. = tablespoon

c. = cup
pt. = pint
qt. = quart

oz. = ounce
lb. = pound

+ + + + + + + + + + + +

3 t. = 1 T.	1 lb. granulated sugar = 2 c.
2 T. = ⅛ c.	1 lb. powdered sugar = 2⅔ c.
4 T. = ¼ c.	1 lb. brown sugar = 2⅔ c.
8 T. = ½ c.	1 lb. sifted flour = 4 c.
12 T. = ¾ c.	1 lb. butter = 4 sticks
16 T. = 1 c.	¼ lb. butter = 1 stick
¼ c. = 2 oz.	1 stick butter = 8 T.
½ c. = 4 oz.	½ stick butter = 4 T.
1 c. = 8 oz. = ½ pt.	¾" of a stick of butter = 2 T.
2 c. = 16 oz. = 1 pt.	⅜" of a stick of butter = 1 T.
4 c. = 2 pt. = 1 qt.	Thin slice of a stick of butter = 1 t.

+ + + + + + + + + + + +

Garlic: 1 medium clove = ⅛ t. garlic powder
Herbs: 1 T. fresh = 1 t. dried
Mushrooms: 1 lb. fresh = 6 to 8 oz. canned
1 lemon = about 3 T. juice

+ + + + + + + + + + + +

+ <u>COMMENTS</u> +

Use regulation measuring cups and spoons from hardware store. All measurements
should be level; level off dry ingredients with back of a knife. When measuring amounts
in quantity, count out loud (so you'll be sure to keep track). Don't try to measure and
talk to somebody at the same time; you'll skip something, or miscount.

+ + + + + + + + + + + +